New Directions for
Teaching and Learning

Marilla D. Svinicki
EDITOR-IN-CHIEF

R. Eugene Rice
CONSULTING EDITOR

Alternative Strategies for Evaluating Student Learning

Michelle V. Achacoso
Marilla D. Svinicki
EDITORS

Number 100 • Winter 2004
Jossey-Bass
San Francisco

ALTERNATIVE STRATEGIES FOR EVALUATING STUDENT LEARNING
Michelle V. Achacoso, Marilla D. Svinicki (eds.)
New Directions for Teaching and Learning, no. 100
Marilla D. Svinicki, Editor-in-Chief
R. Eugene Rice, Consulting Editor

Microfilm copies of issues and articles are available in 16mm and 35mm, as well as microfiche in 105mm, through University Microfilms Inc., 300 North Zeeb Road, Ann Arbor, Michigan 48106-1346.

NEW DIRECTIONS FOR TEACHING AND LEARNING (ISSN 0271-0633, electronic ISSN 1536-0768) is part of The Jossey-Bass Higher and Adult Education Series and is published quarterly by Wiley Subscription Services, Inc., A Wiley Company, at Jossey-Bass, 989 Market Street, San Francisco, California 94103-1741. Periodicals postage paid at San Francisco, California, and at additional mailing offices. POSTMASTER: Send address changes to New Directions for Teaching and Learning, Jossey-Bass, 989 Market Street, San Francisco, California 94103-1741.

New Directions for Teaching and Learning is indexed in College Student Personnel Abstracts, Contents Pages in Education, and Current Index to Journals in Education (ERIC).

SUBSCRIPTIONS cost $80 for individuals and $170 for institutions, agencies, and libraries. Prices subject to change. See order form at end of book.

EDITORIAL CORRESPONDENCE should be sent to the editor-in-chief, Marilla D. Svinicki, Department of Educational Psychology, University of Texas at Austin, One University Station, D5800, Austin, TX 78712.

www.josseybass.com

Contents

FROM THE SERIES EDITOR

About This Publication. Since 1980, *New Directions for Teaching and Learning (NDTL)* has brought a unique blend of theory, research, and practice to leaders in postsecondary education. *NDTL* sourcebooks strive for not only solid substance but also timeliness, compactness, and accessibility.

The series has four goals: to inform readers about current and future directions in teaching and learning in postsecondary education, to illuminate the context that shapes these new directions, to illustrate these new directions through examples from real settings, and to propose ways in which these new directions can be incorporated into still other settings.

This publication reflects the view that teaching deserves respect as a high form of scholarship. We believe that significant scholarship is conducted not only by researchers who report results of empirical investigations but also by practitioners who share disciplined reflections about teaching. Contributors to *NDTL* approach questions of teaching and learning as seriously as they approach substantive questions in their own disciplines, and they deal not only with pedagogical issues but also with the intellectual and social context in which these issues arise. Authors deal on the one hand with theory and research and on the other with practice, and they translate from research and theory to practice and back again.

About This Volume. This issue was developed in response to the problems raised when traditional testing formats are used for courses that have been taught using innovative teaching strategies. The clash is often discomforting for instructor and students alike. The authors in this issue provide both theory and practical examples of what happens when new testing methods are used in both traditional and nontraditional courses.

Marilla D. Svinicki
Editor-in-Chief

MARILLA D. SVINICKI *is associate professor of educational psychology at the University of Texas at Austin.*

EDITORS' NOTES

We decided to compile this volume because of a shift in teaching toward more innovative teaching methods. Anyone in the field recognizes the power of new technologies, new venues, and new students in transforming the learning environments of higher education. However, despite these new teaching strategies, most faculty have been unable or unwilling to move away from the traditional forms of assessment that have been around for so long. Although these assessment strategies have a long history of success in education that is based more on selection than on achievement, we all recognize that they clash with some of the new goals of higher education. For example, as educators, we strive to transfer learning from the classroom to the real world, and yet, the standard forms of testing have little in common with the demands of the environment outside the academy. How many of us have heard the complaint that our students graduate with honors but are unable to make it in the real world?

We also are trying to accommodate a different population of students who come from widely varying backgrounds and who want to make a future that is relevant and gives back to the community. Again, our traditional forms of assessment fail these students. The in-class tests are seen as irrelevant or counterproductive in their eyes.

Although they want to do a good job of assessing student learning, most faculty have not been trained in the basics or new techniques of measurement. Nor were they exposed to new ways of assessing learning in their own educational history. It is unreasonable to expect that faculty can spontaneously produce new forms of assessment for new instructional strategies without a little help. In this issue of *New Directions for Teaching and Learning*, we have brought together examples of alternatives being used in college classrooms today. This issue is directed at faculty who would like some new ideas for student assessment that would give them authentic and valid measures of student achievement but that remain true to good measurement principles.

The first thing we have to concern ourselves with is what the assessment is for—the theories and principles we should adhere to. In Part One of this issue, Susan M. Brookhart (Chapter One) provides a primer on measurement, reminding us (or perhaps exposing some of us for the first time) to what comprises good measurement. J. Ronald Gentile asks (in Chapter Two) an even more fundamental question about whether in any of our classes we test for mastery of the very principles that undergird our discipline.

One of the arguments about assessment today is the need to test the skills that we are aiming for and to increase the probability of transfer of those skills to the real world. All of this falls under the heading of "authentic testing," which is the focus of Part Two. In Chapter Three, Marilla D.

Svinicki provides an overview of the concept of authentic testing with examples of how it might be done. Joseph M. La Lopa shows in Chapter Four how students can be involved in developing the criteria for evaluation, another important aspect of authenticity and an additional way for them to learn. Carmel White (Chapter Five), discusses the use of the increasingly popular method of student portfolios, which have become key in authentic learning settings. Nancy Simpson shows (in Chapter Six) how authentic, creative testing is possible even in an abstract discipline like mathematics. Then the idea of alternative situations needing alternative assessment strategies is explored in a variety of contexts, specifically in performance-based learning by Tim O. Peterson (Chapter Seven) and in laboratories by Judy M. Silvestrone (Chapter Eight).

Part Three introduces the issue of the contribution of technology to testing. Scott L. Howell, in Chapter Nine, explores the contradictory notion that paper-and-pencil tests might be used in classes that are heavily dependent on multimedia. John Kremer shows in Chapter Ten how computer-based testing can be helpful in solving the problems presented by large classes.

In the next three chapters, the increasingly popular but unusual format of group testing is discussed. Linda C. Hodges (Chapter Eleven) describes using group exams in science classes. Theresa R. Castor (Chapter Twelve) provides an interesting twist on group exams by listening to the conversations that occur during them. Karin Sandell and Lonnie Welch (Chapter Thirteen) describe how group testing was implemented in two different courses.

Finally, in Part Five we suggest that testing might be improved by improving the students' ability to take and learn from tests, even in a traditional testing context. Margaret K. Snooks (Chapter Fourteen) reviews preparing students for an exam through the use of extensive pretesting during the initial stages of learning. Michelle V. Achacoso in Chapter Fifteen talks about how to help students learn from a testing experience by analyzing gaps in knowledge and strategy use.

We know that this is not the end of experimentation in testing; rather, it is a beginning. We hope that reading about the innovations of others will inspire readers to experiment with testing in their own settings while still adhering to good measurement principles.

Michelle V. Achacoso
Marilla D. Svinicki
Editors

MICHELLE V. ACHACOSO is coordinator of research and evaluation at the University of Texas Learning Center at Austin.

MARILLA D. SVINICKI is associate professor of educational psychology at the University of Texas at Austin.

PART ONE

Fundamentals of Assessing Learning

Classroom assessment information should be the basis for important classroom processes and outcomes: students' study and work patterns, students' understanding of what they are learning, and teachers' instructional and grading decisions. Attention to principles of assessment quality, especially validity and reliability, increases confidence in the quality of assessment information.

Assessment Theory for College Classrooms

Susan M. Brookhart

Before any evaluation methods are selected and used in a course—alternative methods like those described in this volume or conventional methods like exams and term papers—it is worth stopping to think about assessment theory. Readers of this volume should have less trouble with that assertion than almost any other audience I can think of. Academically trained people recognize that in any field, things do not "just happen." In assessment as in any other field, there are some theoretical principles that will help you organize what you do; separate good practices from bad ones; and especially, recognize, appreciate, and use the information you get from your classroom assessments.

This general introduction to assessment theory, written with the college classroom context in mind, is intended to give you some tools you can use as you apply the assessment methods in this volume and as you find or create other assessment methods. Assessment practices based in sound theory will lead to high-quality information about student achievement in the classroom.

What Is Assessment For?

Assessment, broadly defined, means collecting information about something to be used for some purpose. It is a broader term than *measurement,* which means applying a set of rules (some score scale) to an attribute of something or someone to obtain quantitative information about it (a score or number of some kind). Assessment can include measurement. For example, when you use a multiple-choice exam to measure student achievement of a set of knowledge and skills developed in your course, you typically set up a scale with rules like one point for each right answer. The result is a score that places each student on a scale of achievement. Assessment can also include collecting qualitative information—for example, when you ask a student to describe to you what information from a text he or she found difficult and why. Both kinds of information, quantitative and qualitative, can be useful assessment information. Which to use and why depend on the purpose of your assessment and what you plan to do with the information. Typical classroom assessment purposes include providing feedback to students for their studying, making instructional decisions (what to emphasize in the next lessons and in what manner), assigning grades, and advising students about additional coursework.

Evaluation goes one step further. Evaluation means using assessment information to make judgments about the worth of something. Notice the root "valu" in the middle of the word. Examples of value judgments instructors make based on assessment information include deciding students do or do not know enough about a topic to go on to the next, deciding that a particular lecture or group project was (or was not) worth repeating next year, passing or failing a student, and recommending a student for special work.

If you give a midterm exam and a student scores 64 percent, that is both a measurement and an assessment. If you use that information to conclude that your student should come see you to get extra help or remedial assignments, that is evaluation. If you ask what the problem seems to be, the student's response is also assessment information but not measurement (no numerical scale). Your judgment about the worth of the student's insights is evaluation. Your take on how you should work on the problem together involves both evaluation and instructional decision making—and, one hopes, additional ongoing assessment.

Formative and Summative Assessment

Formative assessment gives assessment information that is useful for continued student learning, positive classroom change, and other improvements. Summative assessment gives assessment information that is useful for making final decisions: for example, assigning end-of-term grades. This sounds like a neat distinction, but in classroom use the boundaries blur, for a couple of reasons. First, formative and summative assessments describe two assessment functions. That is, they describe the *use* of assessment information. Whereas some information is more conducive to being used formatively and some is more conducive to being used summatively, it is the use and not the information that makes the distinction.

The same information can be used for both functions. For example, you might use final exam scores in assigning your course grades and also use them to make modifications to the course content or to the exam itself for the next term. Or you might use midterm exam scores as part of your course grade, and a student might also use the information to change the way he or she studies. If I gave you a copy of a test or a description of a project or paper assignment, you would not be able to tell whether it was a formative or a summative assessment. You would only know that by asking me what I did with the information about student achievement yielded by the assessment. There is evidence that no matter what instructors intend, good students will try to use any information about their achievement in a formative way for their own future (Brookhart, 2001). That is part of what distinguishes good learners.

How Can I Assess the Quality of Students' Work?

To assess the quality of your students' work, you need to know what assessment options are available to you, how to construct or select an appropriate assessment from these options, how to get these assessments to yield good-quality information, how to interpret the information and help students to interpret it, and how to use the information yourself and help students (and sometimes others) to use it. You also need to follow this cycle through to the end so that the information does get used; otherwise, the students' time and yours are wasted.

Types of Assessments. There are four basic ways to collect assessment information (three if you count portfolios as a collection of other assessment methods): paper-and-pencil assessments, performance assessments, assessments based on oral communication, and portfolios. Three different kinds of assessment information feedback can be generated for each: objectively scored numerical data, subjectively scored numerical data, and written feedback. Three types of feedback times four types of assessments gives twelve basic categories to choose from, with a lot of variation within each one! Not to worry, though. Knowing the range of options you have to choose from actually makes deciding on an assessment easier. Once you know what content domain you are assessing and what the purpose is, choosing an assessment becomes a matter of finding the best kind of assessment for its intended use. Then designing the specific assessment is less like staring at a blank screen and more like "writing to specifications."

Assessment Type 1. Paper-and-pencil assessments include objective item tests that use multiple choice, true or false, matching, and fill-in items as well as essay tests. Paper-and-pencil tests are usually given in on-demand settings, as when students "sit for" an exam.

Assessment Type 2. Performance assessments use observation and judgment to assess either a process (how the student does something) or a product (student-created work). Common performance assessments include term papers, academic or technical projects, oral reports, and group demonstrations.

Assessment Type 3. Oral communication is an often-forgotten assessment method. Its most common use in college classrooms is for formative assessment during instruction, when the instructor asks students questions in class.

Assessment Type 4. Portfolios are systematic collections of student work over time, often with accompanying student reflections. The work can be scored as a set; individual pieces of work in the portfolio can be scored; or the portfolio can be used as information for conferences, written feedback, or other communication between instructor and student.

Feedback Type 1. Objective scoring is the kind of one-right-answer scoring that anyone can do with an answer key. Objectively scored items are easy to grade but difficult to write well, and they require more instructor preparation time than subjective items.

Feedback Type 2. Subjective scoring is the kind of scoring that requires judgment. Despite the sometimes pejorative use of the term (as in, "that was so subjective!"), good academic judgment well applied is the heart of a discipline. Thoughtfully applying good rubrics or scoring schemes—ones that use clear descriptions of the work, not just evaluative terms like *excellent, good, fair,* or *poor*—is an effective way to judge quality of complex work (Arter and McTighe, 2001). If possible, share the criteria with students during (and as part of) instruction before the assignment is made.

Feedback Type 3. Written feedback is particularly good for formative assessment. If you describe to a student ways he or she could improve the work, you are providing important information for the student's growing concepts and skills.

Types of Grades, Scores, and Scales. Once you decide that you are going to use quantitative scales because you need numerical data, you need to figure out what kind of scales will give you the best information for your purpose. Again, knowing what your choices are will help.

Test Scores. If you are using a test, decide how many points each item should be worth. Actually, the best way to do it is vice versa: decide how many points each particular course objective should be worth, proportional to its importance or instructional emphasis, and then write the appropriate number of test items. Multipoint essays or show-the-work problems should have some sort of scoring scale, typically either rules for assigning points to attributes of the answer or a rubric (see below).

Analytic Versus Holistic Rubrics. Rubrics are scales, usually short ones, constructed to rate the quality of student work along a series of performance levels described under a criterion. When you apply several scales to the same work—for example, by applying both a rubric for content and one for style to a paper, you are using analytical rubrics. When you make overall judgments on one rubric, you are using a holistic rubric. The same criteria can be used either way, as shown in the example in Exhibit 1.1.

With analytical rubrics, each criterion is considered separately. With holistic rubrics, the criteria are considered simultaneously; to decide where to place a particular piece of student work, select the performance level that *best* describes the work.

Exhibit 1.1. Example of General Analytic and Holistic Rubrics, Using the Same Criteria, for a Question on an Essay Test

Analytic Rubrics (Three Criteria)

Thesis and organization
4 Thesis is defensible and stated explicitly; appropriate facts and concepts are used in a logical manner to support the argument
3 Thesis is defensible and stated explicitly; appropriate facts and concepts are used in a logical manner to support the argument, although support may be thin in places or logic may not be made clear
2 Thesis is not clearly stated; some attempt at support is made
1 No thesis or indefensible thesis; support is missing or illogical

Content knowledge
4 All relevant facts and concepts included; all accurate
3 All or most relevant facts and concepts included; inaccuracies are minor
2 Some relevant facts and concepts included; some inaccuracies
1 No facts and concepts included, or irrelevant facts and concepts included

Writing style and mechanics
4 Writing is clear and smooth; word choice and style are appropriate for the topic; no errors in grammar or usage
3 Writing is generally clear; word choice and style are appropriate for the topic; few errors in grammar or usage, and they do not interfere with meaning
2 Writing is not clear; style is poor; some errors in grammar and usage interfere with meaning
1 Writing is not clear; style is poor; many errors in grammar and usage

Holistic Rubric (Same Three Criteria)
4 Thesis is defensible and stated explicitly; appropriate facts and concepts are used in a logical manner to support the argument; all relevant facts and concepts included; all accurate. Writing is clear and smooth; word choice and style are appropriate for the topic; no errors in grammar or usage
3 Thesis is defensible and stated explicitly; appropriate facts and concepts are used in a logical manner to support the argument, although support may be thin in places or logic may not be made clear. All or most relevant facts and concepts included; inaccuracies are minor. Writing is generally clear; word choice and style are appropriate for the topic; few errors in grammar or usage, and they do not interfere with meaning
2 Thesis is not clearly stated; some attempt at support is made; some relevant facts and concepts included; some inaccuracies. Writing is not clear; style is poor; some errors in grammar and usage interfere with meaning
1 No thesis or indefensible thesis; support is missing or illogical; no facts and concepts included, or irrelevant facts and concepts included. Writing is not clear; style is poor; many errors in grammar and usage

Note: Numbers indicate the points assigned for each rubric.

Source: Adapted from Brookhart, 1999, pp. 47–48. Used by permission.

Analytical rubrics have the advantage of giving more information to both instructor and student. Use analytical rubrics if you want the student to be able to glean diagnostic information by seeing several scores on different attributes of the work. Analytical rubrics have the disadvantage that grading takes longer than with holistic rubrics.

Holistic rubrics have the advantage of speed because only one global judgment is required to arrive at a score. They are therefore better for grading and other summative purposes than for formative purposes. They have the disadvantage of not, by themselves, giving much information about exactly what was thorough or skimpy, clear or unclear, accurate or inaccurate, well reasoned or poorly reasoned, and so forth, about the work.

General Versus Task-Specific Rubrics. General rubrics are those that describe levels of performance for a whole set of similar performance tasks. For example, the rubrics in Exhibit 1.1 can be used with many different essay assignments. General rubrics are recommended because they can be shared with the student ahead of time, thus being part of instruction and also giving students clear information about scoring ahead of time. They take a little longer to learn and to use reliably than task-specific rubrics, but their instructional value is usually worth the trouble. In some senses, you want students to carry around in their heads the definition of general good work found in the rubric; that in itself can be part of the learning.

Task-specific rubrics have elements of the specific problem in them and thus cannot be shared with students ahead of time because they give away the desired answer. An example would be: "Students get a 4 on this problem if they correctly identify Sam as the fastest runner, with a speed of 11.76 minutes, and have one of the following correct explanations (which would be listed)." Task-specific rubrics are easy to use quickly, so scoring is speedy, but you need to write a new rubric for every problem. Use them only when the main purpose of scoring is to ensure that responses contain certain specific facts. Sometimes, instead of a task-specific rubric, it is easier to use a scoring scheme that simply awards points to various required parts of the essay or performance.

Norm- Versus Criterion-Referenced Scales. Any score scale makes an implicit comparison between the work scored and either other students' work (for example, this paper is better or worse than that paper) or some kind of performance standard (for example, this paper has a good thesis logically supported by a variety of evidence and examples). Assessments that yield scores that compare students' work with that of other students are called "norm-referenced" assessments. Assessments that yield scores that compare students' work with a standard are called "criterion-referenced" assessments. For most classroom assessment purposes, you want criterion-referenced scores that tell students how they did with the course material, not other students.

Ordinal Versus Interval Level Measures. Different kinds of scales use different levels of measurement. Rubrics and other, typically short, scales that describe a continuum of achievement quality are ordinal level measures. Test scores and other, typically longer, ways of adding up points for work are interval level measures. This is important because you need to take into account what kind of "data" you will have so you know what you can do with it. The best way to "average" interval level measures is to use the mean. The best way to "average" ordinal level measures is to use the median. If you need to put long and short scales together—for example, for a final grade—you need to find a method that preserves the meaning of the performance information from both scales. Readers who want to learn more about putting different scales together are referred to Brookhart (1999).

Types of Non-Numeric Feedback. Every assignment students do should receive some sort of feedback, but not every assignment needs a score. Sometimes teacher-written feedback (for example, on drafts of essays or preliminary designs for projects) is the most appropriate feedback. Oral feedback can be helpful, too, but with the number of students most instructors deal with, written feedback is recommended. It is difficult to keep too many different comments straight in one's memory! Sometimes other students' responses to the work of their peers make helpful feedback. This can be done orally (for example, in paired or small-group activities in class) or in writing.

Good verbal feedback describes to the student the qualities of the work submitted and makes constructive suggestions for improvement. Good verbal feedback leaves room for student choice in the improvement. I once had a student turn in a report making only the changes I had noted. That was my fault! Instead of writing feedback, I did copyediting. The student did not learn anything further about the qualities of a good report.

How Do I Know My Assessments Give Me Good Information?

Do not make the mistake of believing that alternative assessments are all good or that conventional assessments are all bad, or vice versa. General principles of information quality apply to all assessment information, although these principles may play out a little differently for different types of assessments. For classroom assessment, the two most important indicators of assessment information quality are called validity and reliability (Brookhart, 2003). A third indicator, feasibility or utility, is important in practice, too. An assessment that will take more time than you have, for example, is not much help. Other important assessment qualities include fairness, use of appropriate score scales (discussed above), and appropriate administration and reporting (American Educational Research Association, American Psychological Association, and National Council on Measurement in Education, 1999).

Various authors have recommended ways to collect evidence for the validity and reliability of classroom assessments. What is presented here is not an exhaustive treatment but, rather, practical recommendations about the kinds of evidence an instructor can routinely collect. You will find that if you have evidence that your assessments are valid and reliable, you will feel confident about acting on the basis of their results, whether those actions are formative (for example, going back over an unclear concept) or summative (that is, grading).

Validity. Validity of assessment information refers to its meaning and value. Assessment information should mean what it is supposed to mean. Sound obvious? What about the college course in poetry where much of the term was spent interpreting poems and understanding imagery and then assessed with an exam that had a big "match the poets to their poems" section? The instructor needs a measure of achievement of interpretation and gets a measure of achievement of author-title memorization.

Relating assessment information to course objectives gives important evidence for the validity of your course assessments (Walvoord and Anderson, 1998). This may sound like common sense, but it is important to do thoroughly and thoughtfully. It is not enough to know that the topics on your exams and projects match your course objectives. It is also important to know that the depth of knowledge required and the cognitive level of the tasks (recall or higher-order thinking) match. Finally, the proportions of the various topics and thinking levels on your assessments should go together with the same emphasis you intended for your instruction.

If this all lines up, you will probably find that you have another source of evidence for the validity of your assessments: good consequences for learning and instruction (Moss, 2003). Does your exam point studying to "the right stuff" (as opposed to trivia, or points you did not intend to emphasize)? Does your paper, project, or other assignment result in sharpening the skills (research, writing, and the like) that you intended to teach? Positive intended consequences for learning and minimal negative unintended consequences can be interpreted as evidence for the validity of course assessments.

Reliability. Reliability in achievement measures refers to the amount of confidence you have that the score the student obtained is his or her actual level of achievement. Of course, no measure is perfect. A small margin of error is expected and tolerated. However, if measurement error gets too large, the score information is not useful.

In classroom assessment, there are several reliability concerns, that is, several places where measurement error can creep in. For all subjectively scored work, and for all work where written judgments are rendered, rater accuracy is a concern. Would another person look at the work and draw similar conclusions about its level of quality? Everyone has stories about "easy" and "hard" graders. If the same essay graded by Mr. Smith would yield different information if read by Ms. Jones, that is a problem.

Most of the time, you will not have the time or opportunity to double-score assignments with a colleague (the "acid test" of reliability of scoring judgments). You can maximize the accuracy of your own scoring in two ways: by having clear criteria written out ahead of time and shared with students, if possible; and by using example papers (sometimes called exemplars or anchor papers) or projects for each level of grading.

Another reliability concern is sufficiency of information (Smith, 2003). This one can be easily overlooked, especially in a course with lots to do and where there is little time to do anything twice. If you only ask one question on a test, how do you know that the student's work, whether right or wrong, accurately indicates what he or she can do? Anyone can guess right once or goof once. If you ask several questions about the same course objective, the pattern of student work begins to show—one hopes consistently—what level of work the student can do. Try to have at least five items (or five points) on any one topic before you place too much confidence in conclusions. Rules of thumb are dangerous if applied without thinking; others would say that even more points than five are required for accurate judgments. Probably in a survey course with many topics, the "five-point" rule of thumb is better than no rule of thumb. In more advanced courses that cover fewer topics in more depth, you can do much better than that.

Incorporating High-Quality Assessments into Manageable Classroom Practice

Once you begin to think in terms of the assessment principles laid out in this chapter, it does not take any longer to do high-quality assessments than it does to do poor-quality assessments. And because the information you get from high-quality assessments is better information, in the long run you will actually construct a better course, know more about what your students understand, and be more helpful when they do not understand.

Start with the basic questions, as laid out in this chapter. For every assessment purpose, ask yourself, "What information do I need?" Once you know what you need and why, ask yourself, "What would be the best way to get this information?" Answer your question by thinking through your assessment options and select the one(s) you are going to use.

Then, for each assessment, ask the basic validity and reliability questions: "Would student performance on this assessment really indicate the particular kind of achievement I need to know about?" and "Will I have enough information about each student to be sure about my conclusions?" If the answer to either one is no, adjust before you continue.

And, finally, the usefulness question: In the best case, the assessment information will be useful to you for your purposes (instruction, grading, and so forth) *and* useful to the student as feedback for learning. Sometimes that means you have to provide several kinds of information—for example, both scores and written feedback; sometimes the same information can be used for both student and instructor needs.

The more your assessments begin to provide both you and students with valuable information, the less trauma will be involved. Rodabaugh and Kravitz (1994) did a series of simulation studies and found that a professor who is perceived as fair, especially in testing procedures, will be respected, liked, and likely to be chosen for another class. A professor who is not perceived as fair will not be as respected, liked, or chosen even if he or she gives high grades. Test this out with memories from your own past; the instructors you remember most, and best, were probably not the "easy A's" or the ones who were simply sweet-tempered or charming. They were most likely the ones in whose classes you remember learning something. That learning cannot happen, at least not in a guaranteed manner for all students, without clear, accurate information about achievement—that is to say, without sound assessment.

References

American Educational Research Association, American Psychological Association, and National Council on Measurement in Education. *Standards for Educational and Psychological Testing.* Washington, D.C.: American Educational Research Association, American Psychological Association, and National Council on Measurement in Education, 1999.

Arter, J., and McTighe, J. *Scoring Rubrics in the Classroom.* Thousand Oaks, Calif.: Corwin Press, 2001.

Brookhart, S. M. *The Art and Science of Classroom Assessment: The Missing Part of Pedagogy.* ASHE-ERIC Higher Education Report, Vol. 27, No. 1. Washington, D.C.: George Washington University Graduate School of Education and Human Development, 1999.

Brookhart, S. M. "Successful Students' Formative and Summative Uses of Assessment Information." *Assessment in Education,* 2001, *8*(2), 153–169.

Brookhart, S. M. "Developing Measurement Theory for Classroom Assessment Purposes and Uses." *Educational Measurement: Issues and Practice,* 2003, *22*(4), 5–12.

Moss, P. A. "Reconceptualizing Validity for Classroom Assessment." *Educational Measurement: Issues and Practice,* 2003, *22*(4), 13–25.

Rodabaugh, R. C., and Kravitz, D. A. "Effects of Procedural Fairness on Student Judgments of Professors." *Journal on Excellence in College Teaching,* 1994, *5*(2), 67–83.

Smith, J. K. "Reconsidering Reliability in Classroom Assessment." *Educational Measurement: Issues and Practice,* 2003, *22*(4), 26–33.

Walvoord, B. E., and Anderson, V. J. *Effective Grading: A Tool for Learning and Assessment.* San Francisco: Jossey-Bass, 1998.

SUSAN M. BROOKHART *is an educational consultant based in Helena, Montana, and an adjunct professor at Duquesne University in Pittsburgh, Pennsylvania.*

2

We are all accustomed to periodic summative testing for achievement, but in this chapter the importance of requiring mastery of fundamentals as the baseline for evaluation, regardless of the level of the class involved, is discussed.

Assessing Fundamentals in Every Course Through Mastery Learning

J. Ronald Gentile

Almost every course has several essential objectives that are considered basic or fundamental to the discipline—so fundamental that the failure to master those essentials elicits such comments as "How can one of our graduates not know that?" These essentials range from basic facts or principles to research methods, or from great discoveries in the field to current personalities or theoretical debates.

Given the centrality of these fundamentals to the larger discipline, we might expect them to be central instructional objectives for each course, with periodic assessment to assure that no one squeaks by without mastering them. Often, however, these objectives are so fundamental that we assume they have been mastered, perhaps mentioning them in passing, but mostly taking them for granted.

Assuming knowledge or skill is never as good as assuring it, or at least assessing systematically to distinguish what has been adequately mastered and what has not. In this chapter, I provide a rationale for the assessment of the fundamentals, along with some specific methods for doing so based on principles of mastery learning (for example, Block, Efthim, and Burns, 1989; Gentile and Lalley, 2003). These methods are intended to supplement, not replace, other assessments regularly used in the course. For example, for a second-level or more advanced course, the usual course objectives and assessments may suffice for testing and grading students' acquisition of the new material. Assessing the fundamentals through a mastery learning approach supplements this by testing—and reteaching, if necessary—prerequisite knowledge that may have been inadequately learned or partly forgotten or current information or skills that are prerequisites for later units or courses in the discipline.

The structure of this chapter, then, is first to suggest why a systematic assessment of fundamentals is essential, based on what is known about learning and memory; the advantages of a spiral curriculum; higher levels of thinking; and the distinction between norm-referenced and criterion-referenced assessment. Second, we will consider how mastery-learning principles and procedures can be adopted for or adapted to a particular course to provide systematic assessment of fundamentals to the benefit of both students and faculty. In the last section of the chapter, I discuss these procedures as they relate to the broader goals of classroom assessment.

Initial Learning, Memory, and a Spiral Curriculum

"Learning should not only take us somewhere; it should allow us later to go further more easily." So said Jerome Bruner in his classic book, *The Process of Education* (1960, p. 17). A good curriculum needs to spiral around the great ideas, principles, and values of a field. Thus, our initial learning, which by definition will necessarily be basic and incomplete (but hopefully still accurate), will be revisited later in this *spiral curriculum*. This provides the kind of usable knowledge that Bruner placed "at the heart of the educational process—the continual broadening and deepening of knowledge in terms of basic and general ideas" (p. 17).

The journey of a thousand miles, or instructional objectives, begins with a single step. That step, *original learning,* is usually described as an S-shaped learning curve that progresses from little or no knowledge or skill to an acceptable level of mastery over time. Time needed to achieve adequate original learning varies considerably among learners (see the definition of aptitude in Carroll, 1963, 1989), owing in considerable part to how well prerequisites have been mastered and the number and severity of students' misconceptions.

In addition, because the almost-inevitable result of all initial learning is forgetting, then even initial mastery must be reinforced with additional practice, called *overlearning,* to create synaptic connections (on the physiological level) and allow comprehension and organization of the material (on the psychological level). The good news is that well-learned but forgotten material can be relearned in a fraction of the time required for initial learning—that is, there are *savings* in relearning. Inadequate original learning, in contrast, demonstrates no savings because little or no residue exists in memory. Thus, for overlearning to consolidate accurate and useful memories, original learning must be essentially correct; otherwise, students will be practicing and consolidating their misconceptions.

As the above descriptions imply, a novice's mind is not a tabula rasa, although it may be a sieve. Enter the spiral curriculum, which builds on previous learning in at least two important ways, both of which assume that initial learning was mostly accurate even if not easily accessible at the moment. First, it reviews prior material to allow relearning of its central concepts or procedures in the context of the current instructional objectives. This not only activates prior knowledge but encourages reorganization of that knowledge in the context of the new lessons. Second, a spiral curriculum builds on initially learned concepts, which are usually just the beginning of comprehension or simply memorized facts or procedures, and develops them into higher levels of thinking: other applications, analysis, critical thinking, and so forth (for example, Bloom's "taxonomy of educational objectives," 1956). These two functions of the spiral curriculum may be considered roughly equivalent to what Bruner meant (in the above quote) by "the continual broadening and deepening of knowledge."

Norm-Referenced Versus Criterion-Referenced Assessment

Much assessment in higher education is done for competitive purposes, namely, to compare students' performances for selection into the program or major, for academic awards or rank in class, or for grading on a curve. These are technically known as *norm-referenced assessments* because each person's score is interpreted relative to the performance of others who provide the comparison norms.

Another tradition also prevails in academic settings: setting high standards and then certifying that each student who achieves them has earned the right to be designated or licensed as a professional in that field. This is a *criterion-referenced* purpose, where accomplishments are assessed not in competition with others but rather in relation to specific criteria for what is excellence and what are minimally acceptable levels of competence.

It is my argument in this chapter that, whatever other assessment purposes we may have in a course or program, we must include criterion-referenced assessments for those basic instructional objectives that are so central to the discipline that they inevitably show up in later units or courses. In addition to comparing each individual's performance with some accepted standard, criterion-referenced assessment also requires that we specify and publish the particular knowledge or skills to be learned so that there is no mystery regarding the essentials of proficiency (Glaser, 1963; Popham, 1978; Gentile and Lalley, 2003).

Having abolished mystery learning, we replace it with *mastery learning*. Earning the minimum passing grade in the course becomes contingent on demonstrating mastery of these fundamentals. Higher grades can be earned in other ways: by passing other more competitive tests on additional material, demonstrating higher levels of thinking about the material, or showing creativity or ability to apply the information to other problems or settings. Of course, if at first students do not succeed in passing the mastery test on fundamentals, they must try, try again.

Structuring a Course to Assess Mastery of Fundamentals

The following steps provide a structure for implementing the above ideas (based on Block, Efthim, and Burns, 1989; Gentile, forthcoming; Gentile and Lalley, 2003).

Step 1. Identify the fundamental knowledge and skills in your discipline that are (a) assumed as prerequisites for your course and (b) are expected to be learned in your course (and are therefore likely prerequisites for subsequent courses).

Publish these as mastery objectives or study questions in the syllabus or as a course handout.

Begin the course with a review of the concepts in step 1a, including a test on those concepts within two or three weeks of the semester. This emphasizes the connectedness of the central concepts in the discipline while either refreshing students' memories or giving them an opportunity finally to learn these concepts (if they had somehow missed them). For any student who cannot pass this test at some reasonable level of competence (at least 75 or 80 percent correct), two alternatives seem sensible: students should either drop the course (and enroll in a more basic one or opt for a different field), or they should commit to attend remedial sessions and do whatever is necessary to pass an alternative form of that test or risk failing the course (see step 3).

Following the review of prerequisites, move on to the crucial course objectives in step 1b, emphasizing that passing a similar test (or tests) on those objectives will be required to pass the course.

Step 2. Identify and publish the other objectives for your course—those designed to go beyond the basics but that are required for all, as well as those that are optional or enrichment objectives.

These objectives will be the focus of classroom presentations, discussions, and other assignments alongside the fundamentals (in step 1b), but they will be tested and graded separately as higher-level cognitive processes to organize, apply, or think critically or creatively about the material in the course.

Step 3. Adapt your grading scheme to be clear that the lowest passing grade in the course is earned by demonstrating mastery on both the prerequisite and fundamental objectives in the course (identified in steps 1a and 1b). Build your usual grading scheme on top of that but consider also adding opportunities for students to learn by teaching.

You will need to make a convincing argument (likely in the course syllabus) that passing the fundamentals tests, even with 100 percent correct, earns the lowest passing grade (for example, D or 70). Just as all people get the same driver's license whether they passed the test on three tries or "maxed" the test on the first try, they are still demonstrating only initial competence and will therefore forget what they have learned. Thus, we need to argue (as Gentile and Lalley, 2003, p. 147, put it): "Congratulations, you've learned the basics and are now ready to begin to use this knowledge or skill." That implies overlearning, application, and the development of fluency through the spiral curriculum.

When you think about your own development from novice to expert, your fluency and ability to apply the knowledge easily arose only as you started teaching the material. Bruner (1960, p. 89) quoted a distinguished physics teacher making that point about his difficulty in teaching quantum theory: "I went through it once and looked up only to find the class full of blank faces—they had obviously not understood. I went through it a second time and they still did not understand it. And so I went through it a third time, and that time *I* understood it."

My conclusion: Students will probably have to teach what they are learning before they can truly comprehend or apply their knowledge.

Teaching fellow students should therefore be built into the advanced objectives and opportunity for raising grades. For example, form a cadre of volunteers from among those who passed the fundamentals test to tutor those who need extra help. When the tutored students pass, the tutors earn points or a higher grade as an enrichment project.

The above ideas are not meant to replace the usual activities and assignments of the course. Rather, they are to supplement them and assure mastery of fundamentals.

Step 4. Write several test questions for each mastery objective (in steps in 1a and 1b) and randomly assign them to parallel forms of the tests. Do this before the course begins.

It is virtually impossible to invent a parallel form of a test—that is, one that covers the content in the same way and at the same level of difficulty—after students did not pass your single version of the test. Thus, you must anticipate the need for several versions of the test and write them before you begin the course. This also helps define the fundamental mastery objectives: anything you cannot clearly define or write test questions for should probably be considered enrichment rather than fundamental objectives.

Conclusion

The overarching goal of these procedures is to assure the mastery of a discipline's fundamentals by systematic testing. This has the distinct advantage of emphasizing the centrality of these concepts or methods to the discipline and focusing study time. A further advantage is that many of these fundamentals can be relatively easily assessed by multiple-choice or other objective tests and may even be administered online. A disadvantage is that these mastery tests will likely be perceived as "high-stakes" exams, in that the course grade depends on passing them. Students' anxiety over this can be reduced by scheduling review sessions (for example, by teaching assistants or other students who have passed the test as suggested under step 3) or by requiring students who did not pass to attend remedial sessions to prepare for the next test.

Once a procedure is in place for guaranteeing mastery of fundamentals, then the other, higher-level course concepts can assessed by written reports, essays, performances, portfolios, and other more time-intensive evaluations. Inquiry and critical thinking skills, laboratory procedures, and artistic or athletic skills require performances, which is why such assessments are often called "authentic" (Wiggins, 1989). Whatever else is done to score and evaluate such performances, they also require feedback from a coach or instructor if any improvement is to occur. And coaches everywhere continually speak of the necessity of sound fundamentals for achieving true excellence. Testing for and assuring mastery of fundamentals is a step in that direction.

References

Block, J. H., Efthim, H. E., and Burns, R. B. *Building Effective Mastery Learning Schools.* New York: Longman, 1989.

Bloom, B. S. (ed.). *Taxonomy of Educational Objectives: The Classification of Educational Goals. Handbook 1: Cognitive Domain.* New York: McKay, 1956.

Bruner, J. S. *The Process of Education.* New York: Vintage, 1960.

Carroll, J. B. "A Model of School Learning." *Teachers College Record,* 1963, *64,* 723–733.

Carroll, J. B. "The Carroll Model: A 25-Year Retrospective and Prospective View." *Educational Researcher,* 1989, *8*(1), 26–31.

Gentile, J. R. "Improving College Teaching Effectiveness Via Mastery Learning." In J. E. Groccia and J. E. Miller (eds.), *Enhancing Productivity and Quality in Higher Education.* Bolton, Mass.: Anker, forthcoming.

Gentile, J. R., and Lalley, J. P. *Standards and Mastery Learning: Aligning Teaching and Assessment So All Children Can Learn.* Thousand Oaks, Calif.: Corwin, 2003.

Glaser, R. "Instructional Technology and the Measurement of Learning: Some Questions." *American Psychologist,* 1963, *18,* 519–521.

Popham, W. J. *Criterion-Referenced Measurement.* Englewood Cliffs, N.J.: Prentice Hall, 1978.

Wiggins, G. "A True Test: Toward More Authentic and Equitable Assessment." *Phi Delta Kappan,* 1989, *72*(May), 703–713.

J. RONALD GENTILE, *SUNY Distinguished Teaching Professor of Educational Psychology, retired in August 2004 after thirty-five years with the University at Buffalo, State University of New York.*

PART TWO

Demand for Authentic Assessment Comes in Many Forms

The new learning paradigm brings with it the need for a change in assessment practices as well. In this chapter, one of the assessment practices that is most consistent with this paradigm, authentic assessment, is discussed.

3

Authentic Assessment: Testing in Reality

Marilla D. Svinicki

Recently a significant change has occurred in the types of instructional strategies that are being used in education in general and higher education in particular. Although the lecture-and-discussion methods are still the dominant mode of instruction, some faculty have begun to heed the advice of Barr and Tagg (1995) to move to a learning paradigm in which the learner becomes an active constructor rather than a passive recipient of knowledge. If those who are making the change are doing so because they have actually adopted the philosophy behind the learning paradigm, they must realize that with it comes the need to adopt a new assessment paradigm as well. If instruction is becoming more learner centered, then assessment should head in that direction as well (Anderson and Speck, 1998).

What Is Authentic Assessment?

One of the most commonly occurring changes in assessment that accompany changes in instruction is the move toward more authentic assessment methods. What does it mean to say that an assessment is authentic? It means that the assessment is based on student activities that replicate real-world performances as closely as possible. Assessment is no longer restricted to paper-and-pencil or even computer-drill-and-practice-type tests. Wiggins (1998) provides six characteristics of an assessment that would qualify it as authentic.

1. The assessment is realistic; it reflects the way the information or skills would be used in the "real world."

2. The assessment requires judgment and innovation; it is based on solving unstructured problems that could easily have more than one right answer and, as such, requires the learner to make informed choices.
3. The assessment asks the student to "do" the subject, that is, to go through the procedures that are typical to the discipline under study.
4. The assessment is done in situations as similar to the contexts in which the related skills are performed as possible.
5. The assessment requires the student to demonstrate a wide range of skills that are related to the complex problem, including some that involve judgment.
6. The assessment allows for feedback, practice, and second chances to solve the problem being addressed.

Wiggins also gives a comparison between authentic assessments and typical tests. For example, a typical test "must be unknown in advance to ensure validity" whereas an authentic test "is known as much as possible in advance" because it is based on predictable skills and situations. If the assessment is truly authentic, the kinds of skills it invokes would have been practiced many times before in a wide range of situations so that they become predictable as indicators of learning. He also points out that authentic tests are iterative, "containing recurring essential tasks," whereas typical tests are "one shot." Typical tests have only correct answers whereas authentic tests are aimed more at the quality of the response and its justification. Typical tests sample from the possible universe of testable content, but authentic tests involve integrated challenges that require the learner to assemble components into the final product. Typical tests infer student understanding based on the correlation between what is tested and what is desired; authentic tests go directly to the desired outcome. Typical tests are more summative in nature, but authentic tests provide diagnostic information and feedback to the student so that they can see where and how to make corrections (Wiggins, 1998).

Wiggins does not mean that there are clear lines or a dichotomous categorization of tests as either authentic or not authentic. Instead, he demonstrates that there is a continuum of authenticity along which assessments might fall. For example, he offers the following three scenarios as a demonstration of such a continuum: An inauthentic measure would be to "write a paper on laws." A more authentic measure might be to "write a persuasive essay on why a law should be changed." The difference is the context in which the task is situated and the nature of the task, which is much more realistic because a citizen could conceivably be petitioning for a law to be changed. The most authentic task, however, would be to "write a proposal to present to appropriate legislators to change a current law." Here there is a realistic context and a behavior that is identical to what might occur in life. The difference between the second two is the audience for the assignment. One is still the professor, whereas the other moves the audience to outside the classroom.

This distinction between intended audiences echoes the criteria that had been laid out by earlier experts and that could be used as guidelines for creating an authentic assessment. Newmann, Secada, and Wehlage (1995) listed the following as components of an authentic assessment:

Construction of knowledge
  1. Student organization of information (higher-order skills)
  2. Student consideration of alternatives
Disciplined inquiry
  3. Core disciplinary content knowledge
  4. Core disciplinary processes
  5. Written communications to elaborate understanding
Value beyond the school
  6. Connecting problems to the world beyond the classroom
  7. Involving an audience beyond the school

What Does Authentic Assessment Look Like?

After reading the foregoing descriptions, readers might be saying to themselves that this sounds a lot like what is done in clinical teaching, internships, performing arts, and many other more advanced teaching venues. They would be correct in that observation. There are many fields in which the quality of a student's learning could *only* be assessed in the final performance. Giving a recital or caring for a patient is a classic example of authentic assessment. Can those models be used as the basis for authentic assessment in other fields?

Let us consider some examples of authentic assessments in more traditional settings to clarify what they entail. I have compiled some examples from a range of disciplines, each of which example might be modified for use in other similar settings.

• Snavely and Wright (2003) described their use of a *research portfolio* in an honors thesis course for library students. The portfolio was designed to mimic the information research process used by professionals in the field, including topic definition, search strategy development, database selection, evaluation of resources, an iterative process that involved revision at each step, and teacher and student notes. The portfolio traced the entire process that an informational professional would conduct in the situation of researching a topic for a client. In this case, the students were actually their own clients because the portfolio became the basis for their theses.

• Wellington, Thomas, Powell, and Clarke (2002) described using multidisciplinary teams of students from engineering, marketing, accounting, and industrial design who come together to work on *real-world problems* provided by industrial partners of the institution. The problems involve all the skills that are the target of these programs, including understanding of the problem, design strategies, communications with the client industry, and participation in multidisciplinary teams. The students' work is evaluated by both the instructors and the industry partners.

• Cleveland (2004) teaches a class in management information systems in the University of Texas at Austin McCombs School of Business, a class that enrolls more than eleven hundred students each semester. The purpose of the course is to learn beginning business concepts such as statistics and information management, but applying them to the realities of business can be a challenge. To solve this challenge, Cleveland sets her class up as a *simulated environment*—in this case, a town with groups of students organized as businesses who must develop a business or product idea, go through the process of researching its feasibility in the "town" given its demographics, apply for any pertinent patents or trademarks, and finally, present their business plan at a major business fair at the end of the semester. The groups have to essentially market their business idea to a large group of invited judges representing the town officials and residents. In reality, of course, the judges are invited experts from throughout the university and private sector companies that are sponsors of the business school. Because students in the class come from a range of backgrounds and with a range of skills, they must learn to tap the talents of every member of the group and make the hard decisions that a real business would have to make. The accompanying business plan notebook serves as a record of all that they have done to lead up to the final booth display at the fair.

• Students at the American Film Institute work in teams to create *real products,* in this case, a series of short films, that are then screened by all the faculty and students as well as visiting dignitaries associated with the film industry. Students are drawn from all the components of the institute and represent screen writing, directing, cinematography, set design, and sound. Each student makes a unique contribution to the production, and all must work together to produce the final product.

The foregoing examples are fairly elaborate, but there are much simpler ways of using authentic assessment in classes. For example, most service-learning programs would be considered as candidates for authentic assessment, depending on the type of outcomes the program seeks and the kinds of formative and summative output the students are required to produce. They certainly take place in real environments with real problems, and most use something like a portfolio assessment strategy.

Another example of commonly used evaluation formats ripe for authentic assessment is the research paper. If the paper itself is written for a real purpose other than for the instructor as audience, it approaches authentic assessment. For example, in a sociology class, students might construct a family history based on interviews of their relatives and produce a portfolio that includes old and new photos, interview transcripts, a family tree, and so on. This could even be expanded into a family Web site that includes video clips of family members. The consumers of this product, in addition to the instructor, would be the family itself. The research paper in another format has become the portfolio in which the students display not only the results of their efforts but also the process by which they were achieved and the self-assessment of the success of that process.

In many undergraduate science or science education courses, instructors are beginning to assign projects that involve the production of materials, Web-based or in-class activities, for elementary school use or for dissemination to the public. The college students do the research work to identify an appropriate content, simplify and clarify it for the target age group (the characteristics of which they have researched as well), create the storyboard or the support materials, and package the whole for delivery to local elementary schools or other public venues such as museums. In some cases, the college students even teach their sample lesson to the elementary students or create Web sites that are accessible to the public.

Pluses and Minuses of Authentic Assessment

Much may be said in support of authentic assessment from a technical measurement perspective. Because authentic assessments track the real world so closely, they are likely to have a great deal of face validity both for students and for any outside evaluator. They can also be motivating for students if the students are allowed to choose an assessment type that fits their own interests and skills. Certainly the students will be able to see the value of what they are learning if the product they produce then becomes a reality in public policy or the real needs of people. From a technical psychological perspective, authentic assessments are likely to produce a great deal of transfer from the classroom to the real world after graduation. And having a concrete target at which to aim allows the students to assess their own progress more readily during learning.

There are, of course, almost as many drawbacks to authentic assessment. As with all innovations associated with the new learning paradigm, authentic assessment requires a lot of time and effort on the part of both the students and the instructor. There is probably no real solution to that increased time commitment; it is simply a trade-off for the quality of learning, motivation, and transfer that result from this type of activity.

From a measurement perspective, there are reliability-in-grading issues. Can different works from different students be graded consistently and comparatively? Fortunately, because this type of assessment is becoming more popular and because it echoes the kinds of assessment done historically in clinical or performance venues, much is known about how to improve the quality of evaluation of the products (Palomba and Banta, 1999; Walvoord and Anderson, 1998). A more difficult technical problem is that because no two assignments are identical within a class, it is difficult to make cross-student comparisons. On the other hand, if one is to be consistent with the learning paradigm, you would not be making cross-student comparisons anyway; you would only be comparing a student's efforts with his or her own previous efforts.

Authentic assessment also raises some interesting issues all its own. There are safety issues: When students work in real-world settings, are we putting them or those they work with at increased risk? There are management issues: How much supervision is required, and who should provide it? Who owns the product once it has been finished, the student, the school, or the applied setting? How should it be archived and by whom? The most common form of documentation of such activities are portfolios, which can run into large manuscripts and accompanying materials. There are ethical issues: Is everyone being treated fairly and receiving equal benefit from such assignments, both the students and the individuals they work with? Can students observe the level of professionalism that ensures the privacy and ethical treatment of others? There are student issues: Students who have been highly successful all their student days are now being evaluated on a whole different set of skills and attitudes. Are they ready? Are we ready?

Is It Worth It?

The benefits of using authentic assessments are many, and it is certainly more consistent philosophically with the learning paradigm toward which we are moving in higher education. The pragmatics of designing and implementing these assessments may only be temporary impediments. More and more elementary and secondary schools are moving toward some degree of authentic assessment, however small, despite the press of high-stakes performance testing that is pushing in the other direction. Our students may be coming to expect more because of the real experiences they have already had. Certainly, more is being demanded of us from the public that employs our graduates.

Authentic assessment has the promise to meet this last challenge more than anything that has thus far happened in higher education. What we can measure often becomes what is valued; therefore, we should target our evaluation at what we want valued. It seems far more consistent with our values to evaluate our students in authentic ways so that the real-world skills and attitudes they need become the things we all focus on during their education.

References

Anderson, R. S., and Speck, B. W. (eds.). *Changing the Way We Grade Student Performance: Classroom Assessment and the New Learning Paradigm.* New Directions for Teaching and Learning, no. 74. San Francisco: Jossey-Bass, 1998.

Barr, R., and Tagg, J. "From Teaching to Learning: A New Paradigm for Undergraduate Education." *Change,* 1995, 27(6), 12–25.

Cleveland, L. "Cleveland's Good for Business." University of Texas at Austin Web site: http://www.utexas.edu/features/archive/2004/cleveland.html. Accessed November 14, 2004.

Newmann, F., Secada, W., and Wehlage, G. *A Guide to Authentic Instruction and Assessment: Vision, Standards, and Scoring.* Madison, Wis.: Wisconsin Center for Education Research, 1995.

Palomba, C., and Banta, T. *Assessment Essentials: Planning, Implementing, and Improving Assessment in Higher Education.* San Francisco: Jossey-Bass, 1999.

Snavely, L. L., and Wright, C. A. "Research Portfolio Use in Undergraduate Honors Education: Assessment Tool and Model for Future Work." *Journal of Academic Librarianship,* 2003, *29*(5), 298–303.

Walvoord, B., and Anderson, V. *Effective Grading: A Tool for Learning and Assessment.* San Francisco: Jossey-Bass, 1998.

Wellington, P., Thomas, I., Powell, I., and Clarke, B. "Authentic Assessment Applied to Engineering and Business Undergraduate Consulting Teams." *International Journal of Engineering Education,* 2002, *18*(2), 168–179.

Wiggins, G. *Educative Assessment: Designing Assessments to Inform and Improve Student Performance.* San Francisco: Jossey-Bass, 1998.

MARILLA D. SVINICKI is associate professor of educational psychology and former director of the Center for Teaching Effectiveness at the University of Texas at Austin.

*Authentic learning activities call for understandable
assessments. In this chapter, the process used to involve
students in developing an evaluation tool is described.
This tool was used by a panel to grade proposal
presentations developed in an authentic learning task.*

Developing a Student-Based Evaluation Tool for Authentic Assessment

Joseph M. La Lopa

Sages have said that you never know a thing so well as when you have to teach it to someone else. Let me here add a new coda to that old saying: You know it even better when you have to grade it. That is the essence of this chapter's message. A lot of learning can derive from taking a test, but even more can be achieved when the learners take part in deciding how to evaluate their answers to the test. I came to this conclusion when I decided to take the advice of those who know teaching best and involve my students in an authentic assessment assignment. One of the most difficult parts of authentic assessment is the evaluation and the assigning of a grade. The very nature of the assessment tasks can result in such a wide range of student outcomes that it becomes difficult to predict beforehand what the basis of the grade should be. Before revealing the solution to my problem, I will describe the setting.

In the fall of 2003, I contacted the director of the Lafayette-West Lafayette (Indiana) Convention and Visitors Bureau (LWLCVB) to develop an authentic learning assignment for a senior-level class on tourism business feasibility to be taught in the 2004 spring semester. We brainstormed a variety of projects until one was selected that satisfied both the course description and the immediate need of the LWLCVB. As it turned out, the community had just invested $20,000 into creating a new logo and positioning statement ("Two Great Cities. One Great University") to be used as an overall campaign to stimulate economic development for Lafayette-West Lafayette. The director wanted to have the students submit proposals on how to use the new logo to create a new image for the area for a tourism marketing campaign to attract tourists to Lafayette-West Lafayette. This was an ideal project for the students because they were to learn ways for communities to promote existing businesses or develop new ones to entice people to visit and spend money on tourism-related goods and services and thus boost the local economy.

The overall learning goal for the students taking the class thus became to "create brand awareness through a package, promotion, or marketing effort that will generate economic impact through visitor spending in this community." The project would be no easy task for the students; they were being asked to do something on a par with what the Disney Corporation did with "Mickey Mouse": one look at the icon (logo), and people think of the "family fun" that the company offers through its theme parks, retail outlets, cruise ships, or films. The students would be asked to audit the natural, cultural, historical, and business resources in the area and synthesize them into a single image that comes to mind when people see the new logo, prompting them to visit Lafayette-West Lafayette as a tourist. The students would be required to craft a proposal that explained how they established the logo-image link and present their ideas at the end of the semester to a panel consisting of the director of the LWLCVB, a hotel manager, and the instructor.

This was a worthy project for the class, but their immediate question would, of course, be, "How will we be graded?" Recognizing the difficulty of explaining and achieving consensus on the evaluation of such a complex project, I decided that those being evaluated should have some input into the process. The evaluation tool that was to be used by the panel to grade the proposal presentations would be developed by the students.

Procedures for Developing the Evaluation Tool

Twenty-seven students were enrolled in this senior-level course on tourism business feasibility. Because the class was taught through cooperative learning, the students were allowed to form themselves into seven teams at the beginning of the semester; one team had only three members, but that was okay with the students on it.

As the time for proposal presentations approached, the students were reminded of the course objective pertaining to the development of an evaluation tool: Creating this tool would in and of itself be worth 10 percent of their grade. In addition, the panel of experts would then use their evaluation tool to grade their presentations, which constituted another 10 percent of their overall grade. One week of class time was dedicated to developing the evaluation tool, with minimal guidance from the instructor.

The first step in the development of the evaluation tool was to have students once again review the criteria for the proposals they had been working on during the semester. We wanted to ensure that the panel could properly evaluate the essence of each team's full proposal in light of those criteria. The criteria that had been set for the proposal by the instructor required that it have an analysis of the local market characteristics for

Lafayette-West Lafayette (tourist attractions, demographics, and so on), a comparative–competitive analysis (to see what was unique about the area), projected trends and overall growth for the travel and tourism industry, and new or existing markets that might be attracted to area attractions (along with the size and revenue potential of the segment). The second key section of the proposal would contain each team's recommendation as to one thing that people should think about when they see the logo ("festivals," "performing arts," "outdoor recreation," and the like). The third section would describe the authentic marketing campaign that could be used by the LWL-CVB to promote the logo-image link and entice the intended target markets to visit, spend money, and promote economic benefits. The proposals ended with a section on the estimated return on investment that the community could realize if the intended target markets responded to the new logo-image, visited the community, and spent money at area businesses before returning home.

The students were now asked to reflect on their management and human resource courses on employee and organizational performance evaluations and on any other performance evaluations they had seen or used as part of an internship or part-time jobs while attending school. These reflections should bring to mind employee or business performance evaluations that could be referenced or modified to help the students develop one for their purposes. At the end of class, students were given a homework assignment to consult notes from past courses for evaluations they had seen or used to help them start drafting the evaluation tool for the panel.

During the second class period, the students began working on the evaluation tool under the watchful eye of the instructor. Before taking a seat at the back of the classroom, I suggested that a student volunteer facilitate the discussion of the tool development. The students spent the rest of the class debating the format of the evaluation tool in terms of what should be on it and how the panel could use it to give each team a grade on their presentation. At the end of the class, I asked for another volunteer to type up what the class had developed to that point and bring copies for the next class meeting.

At the beginning of the third class, I questioned the students about the tool up to that point. I asked questions such as: "Do you think the evaluation tool will capture the essence of your proposals?" "Are you using any jargon that might not be understood by the panel members?" "Are the items succinct and measuring what you intend the panel to grade concerning your proposals?" "Do you think the quality of the evaluation tool reflects well on what you have learned after four years of college, or are you just trying to be done with the assignment?" Once sufficiently challenged by these questions, the students dug in a little deeper to formulate a more professional-looking tool that could be used effectively to grade their presentations. It was not an option for the students to develop an evaluation tool that was below "A"-quality work. I could not accept anything less because that would have introduced measurement error among the panelists when grading the presentations. I was prepared to have the students continue to work on it until they had their best effort, worthy of full credit.

The evaluation tool that was developed is shown in Exhibit 4.1. Although the actual size of the evaluation tool was larger to provide more room for comments, the tool shown is a replica of the one used to grade the student proposal presentations. For their work on this tool, the students received full credit.

On the night of the proposal presentations, the expert panel was welcomed by the student teams. The presentations were held at a meeting place owned and operated by the hotelier, who also provided food and beverages. I passed out the evaluation tool that was to be used by the panelists to grade the proposal presentations and provided a brief overview of the evaluation tool so that the director and hotelier would understand its use. The student teams then went through their twenty-minute presentations, allowing five minutes for follow-up questions at the end.

When the evening ended, the panelists compared the grades each had given the seven presentations made by the teams. The tool developed by the students had high inter-rater reliability as evidenced by the similar grades for each of the seven presentations given by each panel member. The tool was also valid in that it captured the essence of each team's full proposal.

Benefits Students Derived from Developing the Evaluation Tool

Having students develop an evaluation tool to help establish part of their grade required them to work through all six of the cognitive levels that are part of Bloom's (1956) "taxonomy of educational objectives": knowledge, comprehension, application, analysis, synthesis, and evaluation.

With respect to knowledge, the students had to *recall* evaluation tools they had learned to use in previous classes or the workplace to have a starting point from which to develop the new tool. With respect to comprehension, they had to *summarize* the tools they had seen before and *explain* them to others while the class was working to draft and finalize the evaluation that was to ultimately be used. Application was demonstrated by the students *taking information* they had acquired in previous settings, either in the classroom or the workplace, and *applying* it to the task at hand. Analysis was accomplished when the students were asked to *compare* and *contrast* the proposal requirements with the evaluation tool they were developing so that the panel would be able to grade the essence of each team's proposal. Synthesis was evident when the students were *creating* the new evaluation itself. Finally, evaluation was accomplished when the students were required to *choose* among alternatives and *judge* whether or not they had produced an acceptable evaluation tool.

Another benefit derived by the students was that in creating the evaluation tool, they at the same time established a standardized presentation

Exhibit 4.1. Evaluation of Brand Proposal Presentations, HTM 499

Thank you for allowing us to present our proposal ideas to you. We would like you to evaluate our proposal using the evaluation tool we have prepared for you this evening. Each item in section A and B is worth 5 points. Please score each item using a scale of 1 (poor) to 5 (excellent). Each item in section C through F is worth 15 points; please score those sections using a scale of 1 (poor) to 15 (excellent).

A. Quality of presentation (5 points each)
   a. Professionalism of presentation   _____
   b. Ability to communicate proposal idea for new logo   _____
   c. Ability to answer panel's questions   _____
   d. Overall quality of presentation   _____
Comments:

B. Quality of proposal content (5 points each)
   a. Clarity of positioning statement   _____
   b. Incorporation of logo into proposed branding campaign   _____
   c. Target market is clearly defined   _____
   d. Trend data support proposal idea   _____
Comments:

C. Marketing strategy is clearly spelled out (total of 15 points)   _____
Comments:

D. Research supports proposal (total of 15 points)   _____
Comments:

E. Accurate budget or adequate return on investments (total of 15   _____
   points)
Comments:

F. Practicality of proposal idea (Total of 15 points)   _____
Comments:

---

format that helped them to take the information contained in their full proposals and boil it down to a twenty-minute presentation. This also helped the panel grade the different presentations objectively and fairly because the presentations conformed to the contents of the evaluation tool.

Conclusion

The process of preparing an evaluation tool to measure their own presentations had many benefits for the students in this class. First, they had to work at all levels of Bloom's taxonomy during the tool development, up to and including evaluation. Such a broad range of challenges created a deeper understanding of both their projects and the overall goal of creating a marketing campaign for a real situation. Second, developing the evaluation tool gave the students a much better understanding of what was required of them. This led to higher-quality presentations and easier, more consistent grading on the part of the evaluators.

An important thing for instructors to remember when using tests and assignments that are authentic is that the skills needed by such assignments are not always clear to the students if they have not been in that situation before. Allowing them to participate in developing the grading criteria for such assignments helps them see what is important and why, which should make everyone's tasks a little easier.

Reference

Bloom, B. S. *Taxonomy of Educational Objectives: The Classification of Educational Goals. Handbook 1: Cognitive Domain.* New York: McKay, 1956.

JOSEPH M. LA LOPA *is associate professor of hospitality and tourism management at Purdue University in Lafayette, Indiana.*

Student portfolios are an alternative authentic assessment method that invites active student learning and provides an opportunity for instructors to tailor assessment strategies based on student-learning outcomes.

Student Portfolios: An Alternative Way of Encouraging and Evaluating Student Learning

Carmel Parker White

The course in which I first used student portfolios was a general education course that required students to learn and apply theories. As is typical for many general education courses, not every student saw the relevance of the course for his or her life and future career. After portfolios were introduced into the course, students took more responsibility for their learning, and I was able to assess their learning and determine if the student learning outcomes had been achieved.

In the first section of this chapter, I describe a student portfolio and how it can be used. Next, I discuss the underlying philosophical approach of student portfolios. In the third section, I outline where the student learning occurs. Students not only learn about a content area and how to apply theories to that content area, but also, and more important, they learn about the process of learning. Finally, I describe the assessment measures I use when grading portfolio assignments. Where relevant, I include comments from classroom research that I have conducted on student portfolios.

Overview of Student Portfolios

Student portfolios, also referred to as learning portfolios (Zubizarreta, 2004), may be used in almost any discipline, may be tailored to fit the needs of many different learning outcomes, and may be in various formats (for example, electronic portfolios are becoming more common). Portfolios can be used to document an entire curriculum or for a specific course. However portfolios are used, it is important to intentionally design assignments to reflect the student learning outcomes of the course or curriculum.

In the general education course that I teach, students work in collaborative learning groups to select a content area to study across the semester. After they have selected a content area, the portfolio assignments center on that content area, and each is due at different times across the semester. Some portfolio assignments vary from semester to semester, and others are consistent across semesters. Portfolio assignments that I consistently use include locating a scholarly journal article, reviewing that article, completing and reflecting on an experiential or community-based learning opportunity, and preparing a group presentation on the topic. Assignments that I have varied across semesters include a critique of an Internet site; an example of what mass media is communicating about this topic; a paper that describes contextual variables that may be influencing this content area, such as one's culture, developmental age, or public policies; a set of survey or research questions that the student is interested in learning more about after being involved in this content area; and a theory-integration paper where students consider the content area in light of a theory or a reflection paper that requires students to integrate their learning across the semester. At the conclusion of the semester, students assemble each portfolio assignment into an attractive package.

Student comments about the assignments I require each semester are included below:

Scholarly article and review. "I think that locating and writing a [review] on the scholarly article was a great way to start the entire portfolio. It made us get out and get started as soon as possible."

Experiential or community-based learning. "I feel that the experiential or community-based learning part of the portfolio gave me the best experience because I was able to understand the applications of my topic (Family Medical Leave Act) on both the employer and employee."

Presentation. "The group presentation provided me with the greatest amount of learning because after we had sifted through the information, decided what was most useful, and prepared the presentation, I really knew the information."

Overall portfolio. "I honestly think every component of the portfolio was helpful and beneficial; especially bringing them all together to present to you."

Underlying Philosophy

Four perspectives have influenced my use of student portfolios. First, the concept of scaffolding, where a more knowledgeable individual holds up or scaffolds the performance of a less knowledgeable individual (Bruner, 1983), thus raising the performance of the less knowledgeable one (not the "sage on the stage" but rather, the "guide on the side"), has greatly affected how I structure portfolio assignments. I find that many students are unsure how to proceed with the task of learning deeply about a specific content area. With each portfolio assignment and my assessment of the assignment, I can guide students through the process of understanding what is a quality journal article, how to critique the main points of a journal article, ideas to think about when participating in experiential or community-based learning, and important issues to be addressed in their presentation. I have included two student comments that support this notion of scaffolding:

> The scholarly article was the stepping-stone for getting my research started and let me know what kind of quality information that you wanted. The review of the article also let me know what style [of information you wanted].

> I think that each portfolio contributed to my learning of [the content area]. Each tied in with one another, gradually increasing my knowledge about the topic.

Another philosophy that has affected student portfolio use in my classroom is the notion that students who select their own content area to research and are allowed to solve problems and discuss issues in an interdisciplinary collaborative learning group are more motivated to learn than they would be if topics were assigned, if they worked in isolation, or if they did not focus on solving problems. For example, one student stated, "We took a subject that I was very interested in (one girl in my group had even been exposed to it) and presented an abundance of knowledge to the class."

A third concept that has informed my use of portfolios is that of student metacognition—that is, helping them acquire an understanding of what they know and what they do not yet know about the process of learning. As Halpern (2003) says, "We always need to remember that we are teaching toward some time in the future when we will not be present—and preparing students for unpredictable real-world 'tests' that we will not be giving—instead of preparing them for traditional midterm and final exams" (p. 38). The following questions become relevant when students complete portfolios: Do students understand what they need to know about the topic and how to gather that information? Are students able to organize a body of information into a meaningful report? Can students reflect and integrate their learning across a body of knowledge? Portfolio assignments can encourage students' metacognitive understanding, as illustrated by this student's comment: "I felt the reflection paper was very helpful. It allowed me to go back over the semester and think about the things I had been involved in, and how I had learned from them."

Finally, the philosophy of authentic assessment has been important in my development of portfolio assignments and corresponding assessments. Authentic assessments are "nearly identical in content and context to the situation in which the information to be learned will be used. . . . What is missing from most authentic situations—and from most real-life situations as well—is *systematic and corrective feedback about the consequences of various actions*" (Halpern, 2003, p. 40, emphasis added). Three student comments reinforce the concept that portfolio assignments allowed for authentic assessment:

> I feel that having to go out and collect an article that is from a reputable source and is still relevant to the chosen topic was a good experience. It is something that will be used in the future.

> Just seeing . . . all the different ways I could take the information I collected and put it into different contexts and still learn a lot about our topic. Plus, it teaches us to be professional.

> I feel that the observation part was where I learned the most. It was the first time I saw firsthand what I had been researching and experienced a real-life situation.

Learning That Occurs

Initially the portfolios were designed to allow students an opportunity to explore deeply a content area and consider how theories could apply to this area. I believe this type of learning does occur, and students realize how much they have learned from different portfolio assignments. For example, one student reported, "Overall, I really enjoyed every single assignment. Every assignment taught me new and valuable lessons about my topic."

However, other types of learning occur while the students are working in collaborative learning groups on portfolio assignments, including peer collaboration, application of content area, and research skills. Indeed, this type of learning may be more important in preparing students for future employment. As Sterngold (2004) stated, "Acquiring strong research . . . skills may be more important to students' future careers than acquiring subject-matter expertise that may become outdated soon after the students graduate or that may become irrelevant when students shift jobs and careers" (p. 19). The following comments reflect students' perception of non-content-related skills that are developed:

Research and Library Skills

> The whole process for the portfolio was very helpful. In my major as a Speech Language Pathologist, I will have to research all the time, and this assignment showed me how and where to get the information.

> Learning how to use a large library was the most helpful part of the portfolio. I am a junior, and this is the first class I have been in that I have had to look up journal articles. That's pathetic.

Application of Content Area

I thought the experiential or community-based learning component allowed me to learn the most. I liked being able to see what we had been learning and reading about in a hands-on situation.

I think the experiential or community-based learning at [social service site] had the most impact on me this semester. To be honest, I've never really been around a lot of "less-fortunate" kids like that.

Peer Collaboration Skills

The group presentation, because my group worked together. We all learned a little so the whole learned a lot. It helped me reach more sources than I could have on my own.

I believe that I learned and received the most from the group presentation. Having others depend on my work made me be more thorough and do a better job.

Assessment Measures

I employ both formative and summative assessment measures on student portfolio use. For formative assessment, I encourage students to provide feedback on their perception of the learning that occurred with portfolio assignments. I collect this type of indirect assessment of student learning at the end of the term about every other semester. The student comments that I have provided throughout this chapter are examples of the formative feedback I have obtained. I use this information to fine-tune the specific portfolio assignments that I use in subsequent semesters and to capitalize on the students' perceptions of what worked well and what could be improved.

The summative assessment measures of student portfolio assignments are the means whereby I assign student grades and provide information to students about the appropriateness of their work for the final portfolio. For each portfolio assignment, I have developed a rubric that outlines the criteria and whether a student's performance is exemplary, good, adequate, or inadequate for each criteria. The following criteria are used for the required portfolio assignments:

Scholarly article. Article is from reputable source, is closely linked to group's content area, and has significant content (substance) to allow you to contribute to your group.
Review of scholarly article. Review demonstrates excellence in grasping key concepts from the article, clearly demonstrates the link between this article and your group's narrowed content area, briefly critiques the article, and may offer alternative interpretations of information presented in the article. Ideas are expressed clearly, concisely; uses appropriate vocabulary.

Experiential or community-based learning. Learning experience must be at least four hours in length, be documented with the contact information and signature of an individual at the site, and describe what you have learned with specific reference to course theories and readings.

Presentation. Each group presentation should contain clearly stated learning objectives for the presentation; have information that is current, in-depth, and well organized; use at least one theory to discuss the content; and be presented in a professional manner.

Overall portfolio. All portfolio assignments should be included and be presented in a manner that would impress a future employer.

These rubrics allow me to assess quickly and intentionally each portfolio assignment and provide corrective feedback to students (Halpern, 2003). For example, if the initial scholarly article does not appear to be from a reputable source or have enough content for the student to use, I require the student to find another article before he or she begins the review of the article.

I have found that student portfolios allow me to assess student learning in an authentic way while intentionally focusing on student learning outcomes for each assignment. Overall, I have been pleased with the quality of learning that is present in student portfolios and what students report that they have acquired in research and peer-collaboration skills.

References

Bruner, J. S. *Child's Talk: Learning to Use Language.* New York: Norton, 1983.

Halpern, D. F. "To the University and Beyond: Teaching for Long-Term Retention and Transfer." *Change,* 2003 (July/Aug.), pp. 37–41.

Sterngold, A. "Confronting Plagiarism: How Conventional Teaching Invites Cyber-Cheating." *Change,* 2004 (May/June), pp. 16–21.

Zubizarreta, J. *The Learning Portfolio: Reflective Practice for Improving Student Learning.* Boston, Mass.: Anker, 2004.

CARMEL PARKER WHITE *is assistant professor in the College of Human Ecology at Kansas State University, Manhattan, Kansas.*

Sometimes a radical shift in assessment procedures may uncover a whole new set of objectives that neither the students nor the instructor expected. Such an experience is described in the context of freshman mathematics.

Alternative Assessment in a Mathematics Course

Nancy J. Simpson

The first principle in the American Association for Higher Education's *Principles of Good Practice for Assessing Student Learning* (reprinted in Walvoord and Anderson, 1998) is that effective assessment practice "begins with and enacts a vision of the kinds of learning we most value for students and strive to help them achieve" (p. 189). Developing the two assessment strategies described in this chapter was and continues to be valuable first and foremost because the process of creating and refining these strategies requires that I clearly articulate for myself the kinds of learning that I most value for my students. It is, of course, important to me that my students walk away from my calculus course with an understanding of the meaning and usefulness of key calculus concepts. It is equally important to me that they grow in their confidence and skill as learners. I structure the course to emphasize their activity, rather than mine. My students read the text outside of class and spend class time asking questions or solving problems (or both) in teams. I assess their learning throughout the course with quizzes, laboratory assignments, writing assignments, and exams. In this chapter, I describe the two components of what has become my final, end-of-semester assessment of their learning.

Context

The assessment strategies described in this chapter occur in the context of an honors calculus course that satisfies a core-curriculum requirement. The course is a one-semester calculus course designed for students majoring in the liberal arts or life sciences. It generally enrolls twenty students. Most, but not all, of the students are in their first year of college. The students are divided into four-person teams and work with their team on in-class exercises and team quizzes throughout the semester.

Motivation

Traditional assessment in most mathematics courses involves quizzes, exams, and problem sets, and during the first several years that I taught this one-semester honors calculus course, I used all of these familiar methods of determining what my students have learned. The statement on my syllabus was familiar—and therefore comfortable—for both the students and for me: "Your grade in this course will be based on total points earned on weekly quizzes and problem sets, three unit exams, and a cumulative final."

The semester that I began to experiment with an alternative to the cumulative final was a semester that I had a particularly bright and gregarious group of students who began lobbying good-naturedly for an optional final. They pointed out (correctly) that they had already been tested on all of the material in the course and argued that a cumulative final exam would be redundant. I responded that the department strongly discouraged optional finals and that the point of a cumulative final was to see if they could remember and put together all the material on which they had been previously tested. This last claim rang a little hollow even in my own ears, particularly the notion that they would be required to "put together" material from previous exams in response to new problems. I had to admit that my cumulative final exams were merely a compilation of problems that could have appeared on any of the individual unit exams; no true synthesis of concepts was required. This exchange with my students, and the reflection that it stimulated on my part, resulted in the creation of the "visual synthesis," a form of final assessment that I continue to use whenever I teach calculus. The visual synthesis is described in the next section of this chapter.

Because the visual synthesis is a team activity and because I wanted to have some means of assessing the learning of individual students in my course, I have begun to use a second alternative form of assessment in my calculus class: the "learning portfolio." Learning portfolios are not new, and they are being used with greater frequency as a form of assessment of student learning outcomes within academic programs (Zubizarreta, 2004). My personal path to the learning portfolio as an assessment tool in my calculus class emerged from many years of working with faculty on the development of teaching portfolios. That work has taught me that both reflection and documentation are important to any professional or personal development process (Simpson and Layne, 2004). In the third section of this chapter, I describe my adaptation of the learning portfolio as an assessment of individual student learning in my calculus class.

Visual Synthesis

The first component of my move toward more meaningful assessment of my students' learning was the requirement that they produce a visual synthesis of their understanding of the course concepts.

Initial Implementation. When I announced the visual synthesis to that first group of students five years ago, my instructions were somewhat lacking in detail—both by design and of necessity. I wanted to see what the students would create without a lot of explicit instruction, so I deliberately kept my description loose and open-ended. And, because this was a new idea for me, I honestly did not know exactly what a "successful" product would look like. What I told my students was this: "On the day of the final, I will bring flip-chart paper and markers. Your mission is to create a visual depiction of what we have learned in this course over the past semester. You will want to capture the major concepts as well as the ways in which those concepts are connected. You will have the first hour to create your visual, and during the second hour each team will present its work."

My students responded positively to this assignment, and the results, for the most part, exceeded my expectations. They clearly had fun being creative and later enjoyed seeing the variety in the visualizations produced by the five different teams. Although they described this as a "low-stress" final, they also reported spending more time preparing for it than they would have spent studying for a traditional final exam. The creations from that first year hung in my office for decoration and inspiration for several semesters, but they now live only in my memory. A brief description of some of their projects is found in Exhibit 6.1.

Current Use. I have used the visual synthesis as one part of the final assessment in my honors calculus course for four semesters now. Each year's experience has contributed to the evolution of the instructions that I give my class. (The most recent iteration of these instructions is found in Exhibit 6.2.) I learn from both my students' successes and their failures. For example, the one disappointing product the first year came from a team that included a talented artist. This team's artwork was elaborate and beautiful, and the group talked about some of the concepts they had learned while they gave a tour of the pictures, but the project itself contained no mathematics. Now I warn the students about this. I tell them that I invite and encourage their creativity, but that the mathematics is the most important part of their project. An example of learning from student success comes from my most recent use of the visual synthesis during the spring 2004 semester. Although not an explicit requirement, each of the groups in this class chose to make up a real-world application that they would be able to use as the connecting thread for their project. During my questioning of each team, I asked, "What was most challenging?" and "What was the most important discovery that resulted from this project?" All of the teams, in

Exhibit 6.1. A Sample of Student Work Resulting from the Visual Synthesis Assignment

Calculus Theme Park
Visitors to this theme park entered through *function land* in which the rides took the shape of the several categories of functions we studied in the foundational unit of the course: linear, power, exponential, periodic, logarithmic. The descriptions of the rides conveyed the students' understanding of the characteristics of the functions. The rest of the theme park was divided into *graph land, algebra land, number land,* and *word land,* reflecting our emphasis on the "rule of four" or the representation of concepts graphically, algebraically, numerically, and verbally. In each section, the major concepts of the course were given the appropriate representation and explanation. The train that ran around the entire park, connecting it all, was labeled the Fundamental Theorem of Calculus.

Whoville and New Whoville
One of the members of this team was a Dr. Seuss fan, hence the theme of the project. Differential calculus was depicted in Whoville, with the inhabitants of Whoville carrying out various tasks that were explained by or made use of the concepts of the derivative, limit, continuity, and optimization. Something catastrophic happened, requiring the village to recreate itself in New Whoville, where integral calculus was depicted. But Whoville was not forgotten: a bridge connecting the two villages was labeled the Fundamental Theorem of Calculus.

The Tree of Calculus
This project was clearly inspired by the fact that we often refer to the "branches" of differential and integral calculus. The categories of functions studied in the foundational unit of the course were represented by the roots of the tree. The trunk was labeled the Fundamental Theorem of Calculus, and the two major branches of the tree represented differential and integral calculus, with the associated concepts described or illustrated on the leaves of the tree. This team also included other aspects of learning such as teamwork (the sun) and exams (the rain) that helped the tree grow and problem-solving abilities (birds nesting) that were encouraged (sheltered) by the tree.

answer to one or both of these questions, talked about the real-world application. They found it challenging to find something realistic that they could describe with the mathematics they had learned. In many cases they said something like, "Being able to apply this to something that I am interested in made calculus make more sense to me." This appeared to be such a valuable part of the project that I intend to make it an explicit requirement in the future.

Evaluation of Student Learning Through the Visual Synthesis. Not surprisingly, evaluation is the most challenging part for me as an instructor. However, as my instructions and expectations for the visual synthesis have become more clearly defined, evaluation of the resulting student work has become less difficult. During the second hour of the final exam period, I walk around to all of the groups and ask them to "give me a tour" of their project. Depending on the project, I may ask some clarification questions,

Exhibit 6.2. Instructions for Visual Synthesis

Your *goal* for the visual synthesis is to convince me that you are walking away from this course with a thorough understanding of the basic concepts of calculus. Your *task* is to create a visual representation of what you have learned about calculus during this past semester. Your visual should communicate (1) the key concepts of calculus and their meanings, (2) the connections between and among these key concepts, and (3) the ways in which these key concepts might be applied.

You will have two to three class periods during which you may work together to plan your visual synthesis, but you will probably need some additional time outside of class to work together on this. On the day of the final, I will bring flip-chart paper and markers. You will have one hour to create your visual synthesis. During the second hour, your projects will be displayed for all of us to look at and ask questions about. Each person on the team should be prepared to answer questions about any part of your project. Evaluation of your project will be based on *completeness* (are all of the key concepts of calculus included? Is there sufficient detail to convince me that you understand the meaning and usefulness of the concepts?), *connections* (does your project communicate the connections between and among the concepts?), *explanation* (is each member of the team able to answer questions and explain the different elements of your visual synthesis?), and *creativity* (have you found a creative and appropriate way to communicate what you have learned?).

and then I ask the global questions described above. I then take all of the projects back to my office, spend more time reading each one in detail, and use a rubric (see Table 6.1) to guide my evaluation. The component of the rubric with which I am not yet satisfied is "explanation." This dissatisfaction stems from the fact that there is insufficient time during the presentation hour to ask questions of all members of all groups. An approach that I may try in a future semester is to look at the projects while they are being constructed (during the first hour), write questions about each project, and have each team member draw a question to which to respond in writing.

Benefits of the Visual Synthesis. As the name I have given this alternative assessment implies, the greatest value of the visual synthesis lies in the fact that students must synthesize what they have learned in small chunks throughout the semester. Rather than simply refresh their memories about the small chunks, they have to step back and ask themselves, "What is calculus about? What are the most important concepts? How do they connect? What are the best ways to illustrate these concepts and connections?" They spend time both in and out of class preparing, and they supplement and reinforce each other's learning by their conversation. Because I do not give a traditional cumulative final, I cannot compare evidence of student learning found through this assessment tool with that through a traditional exam. However, the students report that the visual synthesis leaves them with a better sense of what they have learned than they think would happen with a traditional final exam. Sample student comments are found in Exhibit 6.3.

Table 6.1. Rubric for Evaluation of Visual Synthesis

Category	4	3	2	1
Completeness	The following concepts are represented with sufficient detail to convince viewer that team understands meaning and usefulness of concepts: Derivative Definite integral Indefinite integral Limit Fundamental Theorem of Calculus Instantaneous rate of change Local or global maximum or minimum points Other	Most but not all of the key concepts are represented with sufficient detail	Most of the key concepts are represented but not all with sufficient detail	Three or more key concepts are missing, and those that are represented do not have sufficient detail
Connections	The visual synthesis indicates the connections between the limit concept and the derivative or definite integral concepts; between the derivative and the local or global maximum or minimum; between the definite and indefinite integral; the role of the Fundamental Theorem in connecting the two branches of calculus	Most but not all of these connections are depicted	Few of these connections are depicted	No connections are depicted
Explanation	Each person was able to answer questions directed at her or him without help	Each person was able to answer questions directed at him or her but sometimes needed help from teammates	At least one person was unable to answer questions regarding the project	Two or more people were unable to answer questions regarding the project
Creativity	The visual images selected to represent concepts and connections are creative and appropriate to the ideas that are being communicated	The visual images selected contribute to the communication of concepts and connections but are not particularly creative	The visual images selected to represent concepts and connections are creative but do not contribute to the communication of ideas	The visual images selected are neither creative nor appropriate to the ideas being communicated

Exhibit 6.3. Student Perceptions About the Visual Synthesis and Learning Portfolio

"I took more time on this project and preparation of my portfolio than I would have likely taken to study for the traditional final."

"I think this project was extremely effective because as I was doing it, I thought that I really was putting all the pieces together and studying for the final."

"At the beginning of the project, I wished I could just take a final and get it over with. However, during the project, I realized that I was actually getting a better understanding of the concepts and how they related to each other than if I had simply tried to study for a final. The group project and portfolio were a great way to tie all of the things I learned together and leave them imprinted in my mind."

"I enjoyed the team project and learning portfolio. In a way, it was good to see the visual synthesis because it demonstrated the relationships between all of the concepts we have learned this year. The portfolio served as a good review of all the concepts."

"We would rather have done one or the other, but we can see more clearly the growth we have had from the different projects. It was hard not to include our group presentation in our portfolio because it was truly an accumulation of everything we have learned. We developed stronger group skills, and this approach caused us to have a 'backward' view of the concepts. These projects helped us all gain a greater understanding of calculus."

"I really liked the visual synthesis, which gave us a chance to have fun with math. I found the portfolio challenging because of its open-endedness. I'm one of those people who prefer explicit instructions. On the other hand, the challenge was good because it really made me think about what I had learned—what was new, difficult, etc. . . . There's not a whole lot that I would change, just stress that it is *time-consuming*. I think a lot of us thought it wouldn't take as long as it did!"

"Putting together the learning portfolio probably took more time than studying for a final, but it really helped me realize how much I have learned."

"I realize the difference between honors and non-honors now. I liked doing this because I love writing and I explain and understand much better through words, so this works for me pretty well. I also loved doing something a little different by writing a poem."

Learning Portfolio

I assigned a learning portfolio for the first time during the spring 2004 semester. In this section I briefly describe what I asked students to do, the results, and plans for revising the process.

Description of the Process. I modeled my guidelines for the learning portfolio (Exhibit 6.4) on the guidelines that the Center for Teaching Excellence at Texas A&M University has developed for faculty teaching portfolios (Simpson and Layne, 2004). Both types of portfolios involve reflection and documentation. For the learning portfolio, I asked students to write a reflective essay describing their growth over the semester in four categories: calculus concepts, calculus skills, problem-solving abilities, and learning

Exhibit 6.4. Guidelines for Math 131 Learning Portfolio

Description of Portfolio
The portfolio is an excellent method of demonstrating what you have learned in a class. An important part of the learning process is reflecting on what you have learned, how you have learned it, and how you know that you have learned it. The process of putting together a learning portfolio will facilitate this reflective process and allow you to describe and document your learning.

Your learning portfolio will have two components: (1) a reflective essay that communicates your description of what you have learned this semester in Math 131, how you have learned it, and how you know you have learned it; and (2) a set of documents that illustrate what you describe in your reflective essay. The reflective essay is described in more detail below. Possible illustrating documents are listed in the last section of this handout.

Reflective Essay
Using the questions below as a catalyst, reflect on your learning experience, with special focus on these four areas: *calculus concepts, calculus skills, problem-solving abilities,* and *learning abilities.* The questions below will get you started, but I encourage you to use these only as a starting point. As you consider the quality and quantity of what you have learned, remember to refer to your supporting documents as evidence of this learning. For example, you might write that "The first CPR assignment required me to _____, and by doing this, I understood _____ more clearly. This is illustrated in Appendix 1, where you will see my original CPR text along with a revised CPR text and my description of what changes I made and why I made them." The above example refers to a specific area of improvement or learning and relates it to a document that illustrates that learning. The more concrete your illustrations, the better.

Calculus Concepts
What are the major calculus concepts that I have either learned for the first time or learned at a deeper level? What do I understand now that I did not understand at the beginning of the semester? What concepts were difficult to understand? How do I know that I understand these concepts? Have I improved my ability to articulate the meaning of these concepts? Have I recognized these concepts when they come up in other courses or in my everyday experience?

Calculus Skills
How confidently can I find derivatives and integrals of all kinds of functions? Am I able to analyze functions using information from the function itself as well as from the first and second derivatives? Am I able to use the "rule of four" fluently? Have I learned to find and use regression equations? Have I learned to recognize basic functions, and do I know their graphs, domain, range, and so on?

Problem-Solving Abilities
Am I willing to explore and persevere with a problem that I have never seen? Have I gained confidence in applying calculus concepts and processes to new situations? Have I learned to solve problems involving exponential growth and decay, minimization or maximization questions, or questions about an area under or between curves?

Learning Abilities
What have I learned about myself as a learner? Have I grown in my ability to formulate and ask questions that help me deepen my understanding? Have I identified my learning strengths? Have I identified my weaker learning styles and found ways to strengthen them? Have I developed skills in working and learning with other people? What learning activities did I respond to most easily? Why? What learning activities did I find most difficult? Why?

Exhibit 6.4. (Continued) Guidelines for Math 131 Learning Portfolio

Illustrative Documents
These should be selected from all of the work you have done this semester, for the purpose of illustrating what you write in your reflective essay. Possibilities include reading quizzes; in-class exercises or quizzes; CPR assignments; labs, exams; examples of calculus or related concepts from other courses, newspaper articles, and the like; e-mailed explanations to friends; analysis of before and after self-assessment; copies of your reading notes; other work that you may do specifically for this portfolio; *revisions* to CPR assignments; quiz problems; exam questions; and so on.

Format
The format that you choose for presenting your portfolio is up to you. A three-ring binder with dividers is one option. Those of you who prefer electronic formats may wish to do something with a Web page or other electronic means of presentation. You choose a format that works best for you.

How Will I Evaluate Your Learning Portfolio?
 1. Completeness (30 points)
      a. Have you addressed all four areas of interest?
      b. Within the areas "calculus concepts" and "calculus skills," have you included all of the key concepts and skills that we have covered this semester?
      c. Have you included documents that illustrate the points you make in your reflective essay?
 2. Depth of reflection (30 points)
      a. Does your reflective essay go beyond surface statements and demonstrate that you have examined not only the "what" but the "how" and the "why" of your learning?
      b. Does your portfolio demonstrate growth?
 3. Organization and readability (10 points)
      a. Is your portfolio organized in a way that makes it easy to read and understand?
      b. Is your reflective essay free of mechanical (spelling, grammar, and the like) errors?
 4. Above and beyond (5 points or more)

This is an honors class and you are all highly motivated and bright students. I include this last section so that you will have the opportunity to surprise me—to include things that I have not explicitly asked for.

abilities. I asked them to document the statements that they made in their reflective essay with samples of their work from the semester. I gave them questions to serve as a catalyst for their thinking for their reflective essay, and I gave them suggestions for documentation. Some of the students were uncomfortable with the open-endedness of the assignment, and several asked if they could see samples from previous years. Because I had never before assigned a learning portfolio, I obviously could not provide samples, and I allayed student anxiety with "I'm sure you'll figure it out" or words to that effect.

Results. The students did, in fact, "figure it out." Although I had been warned by colleagues that I would likely be disappointed ("first-year students do not know how to be reflective"), I was anything but disappointed with the results. Each student put his or her own spin on the portfolio assignment. One student wrote a poem, another created a Web page, and still another made a scrapbook. In all cases, they wrote careful, thoughtful essays about what they had learned and how they had grown and provided documentation in the form of samples of the work they had turned in throughout the semester.

Plans for Revising the Process. Although I was satisfied with the results of the learning portfolio assessment this past semester, I plan to make three changes when I teach this course again.

To encourage students not to leave the creation of the portfolio to one marathon session at the end of the semester, I will set up checkpoints along the way. Although I strongly encouraged them to work on the portfolio in small chunks, none of the students did so. This left them with a major task to complete at the same time that they were working on their visual synthesis and studying for other final exams.

I will require that the documentation include revision of work done during the semester. This semester, I listed this as one possible piece of evidence of learning, and a few students included it, but most did not.

I will explicitly ask the students to include an analysis of their preassessment survey. On the first day of class, I do a preassessment review to get a sense of what students perceive that they already know about calculus. On the day before the final, I returned the preassessment survey with the explanation "just in case you want to include this in your portfolio." Several of the students did include it, and their comments indicate that it was useful to them to look back and see what they wrote at the beginning of the semester so that they could see how far they had come.

Conclusion

Traditional forms of assessment (quizzes, exams, and problem sets) are an important mechanism for finding out what students can do mathematically, and these will always be a part of mathematics courses that I teach. The additional assessment processes described in this chapter will also remain a permanent part of my repertoire of strategies for assessing students' learning. Whereas the former tell me what students can do in response to the questions and problems I pose, the latter require students to ask the questions themselves: What have we learned? What are the big ideas of calculus? What exam questions tested understanding of specific concepts? Which problem set demonstrated that I can write a careful and correct solution to this kind of problem? What new knowledge and ability am I taking with me from this course? Asking these questions is part of being a good learner, and part of my objective as a teacher is to help my students become good learners. The visual synthesis and the learning portfolio help me to accomplish that objective.

References

Simpson, N. J., and Layne, J.E.L. "Teaching Portfolios at Texas A&M University: Reflections on a Decade of Practice." In P. Seldin (ed.), *The Teaching Portfolio: A Practical Guide to Improved Performance and Promotion/Tenure Decisions.* (3rd ed.) Bolton, Mass.: Anker, 2004, pp. 92–100.

Walvoord, B. E., and Anderson, V. J. *Effective Grading: A Tool for Learning and Assessment.* San Francisco: Jossey-Bass, 1998.

Zubizarreta, J. *The Learning Portfolio: Reflective Practice for Improving Student Learning.* Bolton, Mass.: Anker, 2004.

NANCY J. SIMPSON *is director of the Center for Teaching Excellence and lecturer in the department of mathematics at Texas A&M University, College Station.*

Problem-based service-learning projects are complex and ambiguous learning environments. New thinking about assessment must occur to be able to assist the learning from this type of project.

Assessing Performance in Problem-Based Service-Learning Projects

Tim O. Peterson

Shortly after the crisis of September 11, 2001, I proposed the development of a class called "Crisis in Organizations." As part of this proposal, I suggested that a significant part of the class revolve around a problem-based service-learning project. This would require integrating the problem-based learning instructional method with the service-learning instructional method. Problem-based learning can be defined as "the learning that results from the process of working toward the understanding or resolution of a problem" (Barrows and Tamblyn, 1980, p. 18), whereas service learning is defined as an instructional method that combines valuable community service with classroom instruction where academic content, community action, and self-reflection are integrated (McCarthy and Tucker, 1999). Combining these two alternative learning methods would provide an ambiguous and complex learning environment, like the environment that contains potential or actual crises.

The concept was to have the students engage in actual crisis prevention and preparation activities for a real organization in the community by providing them with knowledge, ability, and feedback that would allow them to be effective in resolving the problem presented to them by their client. The class was designed as an elective in the College of Business at Oklahoma State University (OSU), which offers classes in Stillwater, Tulsa, Oklahoma City, and other locations. The class was open to all graduate students. The first offering of this class (spring 2002) had twenty students enrolled at the Tulsa campus. The students worked on five different potential crises identified by senior administration at OSU-Tulsa. These projects or problems included grade tampering, bankruptcy or departure of

NEW DIRECTIONS FOR TEACHING AND LEARNING, no. 100, Winter 2004 © 2005 Wiley Periodicals, Inc.

one of the major business organizations in the local area, a campus building being destroyed by a tornado, a hostage situation, and an accident involving a university-owned shuttle bus that transfers students and faculty members between Stillwater and Tulsa. In the spring of 2003, the class was offered both at the Stillwater campus and at the Tulsa campus. Nine more projects (five in Stillwater and four in Tulsa) were completed. The value of these fourteen projects to the organizations was estimated to be $350,000.

From many different angles, this class was viewed as a success. First, it demonstrated the responsiveness of the Department of Management, College of Business, and the university to an immediate need for crisis planning that was realized after September 11. Second, it better prepared the organizations for potential crises they might face. Third, it saved over three hundred thousand dollars for these organizations. Fourth, the students took away important crisis knowledge and abilities to other organizations. The Tulsa students are working professionals who have applied what they learned in their workplaces. For example, one of the former students of this class is finalizing a major rewrite of an organization's disaster-preparedness plan. Other former students have said that they are helping to update their organizations' emergency-response plan. Another former student said that her recent job hire was a result in part of her knowledge of crisis prevention, preparation, and response. However, hidden in all of these successes is another success. This success was the use of alternative assessment practices that enhanced and directed the learning in this class.

In the remainder of this chapter, I want to focus on three alternative assessment practices. Two of these practices have been written about in previous publications (Anderson, 1998; Smith, 1996, 1998) but still need emphasis and enhancement. These two alternative assessment practices are assessing the task work (product) and teamwork (process). The third alternative assessment practice has received little to no attention, and yet, the phenomenon always appears in problem-based service-learning projects. This phenomenon is unexpected or serendipitous behavior by the project team or a project member as they go about resolving the problem facing them. These unexpected and serendipitous behaviors can be either negatively deviant or positively deviant (Cameron, 2003). They can be either ineffective or excellent, inefficient or extraordinary, or error-prone or flawless. But no matter what, these unexpected and serendipitous behaviors must be recognized and assessed if we are going to assist our students in the learning process. In this chapter, I describe all three alternative assessment practices.

Assessing Task Work (Product)

All problem-based service-learning projects have a task that must be accomplished. Often the final product of this task work is in the form of a report and oral presentation. One significant factor in service-learning projects is that this product is for a real-world client. These clients are expecting a quality product to help answer a pressing problem they are facing. Because the final product is to be delivered to a client, assessment cannot be left until the summative phase. An alternative formative assessment must be developed. However, my past experience demonstrated that if there is no payoff (points) assigned to the formative assessment, the quality of the initial product is poor, and it wastes the time of both the students and the professor.

Over a few years of experimenting with methods to assess the task work, I have realized that it is important to be able to provide critical but informative feedback without de-motivating the students. I now allocate 10 percent of the total assigned points for the specific task to the initial version of that product. For example, if the project calls for a final report, I would ask for a completed copy of the final report two weeks before it is due to be turned over to the client. Therefore, let us assume that the final report is worth 1,000 points. I would assign 100 of those points to the initial version of the report. This copy of the report would receive a thorough review. The goal is to find everything that is wrong with the report. This includes formatting, grammar, spelling, reasoning, conclusions, and anything else the project requires. I document all mistakes, problems, and flaws on the copy turned in by the team. I will take off as many points as necessary to assist the students in seeing and understanding the deficiencies in their report. The report is returned to the student team within twenty-four hours of my receiving it. Now, if the students take my comments and improve on their report, they still can earn enough points to receive an A on the final report. Whether we like it or not, Anderson (1998) is correct that what gets assessed is what gets attention. In addition, the students know that their report will be a better final product that they can be proud of when they deliver it to their client.

If an oral presentation is required, I follow the same process. Ten percent of the final presentation grade is assigned to an initial presentation made to me and the other members of the class. This initial presentation accomplishes two important goals. First, it gives the group the chance to practice the presentation with some pressure because they have an audience. Performance actually improves when there is a moderate amount of stress involved (Csikszentmihalyi, 2003; Hellriegel and Slocum, 2004). Second, it allows me to make sure that the group is not going to say anything that would be inappropriate. For example, in one of the practice presentations, the group began by saying, "This work unit is all screwed up. So, our first recommendation is that you fire Fred Jackson." Although termination might be the right thing to do, politically it is not the right thing to say at the start of a presentation. After they completed their presentation, I asked if they knew if Fred was going to be present at the final presentation. They said they did not know. I asked, if he was going to be there, how did they think he might respond to their presentation? They agreed that he most likely would be defensive and that he might try to undermine or sabotage the presentation. This practice presentation and my formative evaluation gave the group the chance to reconsider how they were going to present their findings in a more acceptable manner. It also allows the university to maintain a professional and positive working relationship with a community organization.

Assessing Teamwork (Process)

Anderson (1998) points out that alternative assessments measure more than just the product. They also measure the process. In problem-based service-learning projects, the process involves the teamwork that must occur. Smith (1998) says that many of the problems related to cooperative projects can be eliminated by carefully structuring the group and by providing both formative and summative assessment of the team process. In another article (Peterson, forthcoming), I write extensively about how to structure the team. Here I will focus on the assessment process.

Three critical aspects of the team process need to be assessed to assist the team with the process. These are the team's core values, the team's purpose, and the team's performance management system. All of these attributes should be assessed using a criterion-referenced assessment method. Smith (1998) defines a criterion-reference assessment method as setting an absolute standard for earning a specific grade. Table 7.1 shows the criterion-referenced guide I have developed for these types of projects. This criterion is published in the "Team Project Policy and Procedures Manual" that all of the students receive. It makes it clear that every team can receive an A if the work of the team meets the specified standard, but it also makes clear that if none of the teams meet the standard as specified in the guide, then no team will receive an A.

Most students are initially puzzled about why they are being assessed on the team process. They have generally been put in groups, but the process that they use to produce the product has generally been ignored in the assessment process. The students have come to believe that the process is unimportant and that the only thing that is important is the finished project. If we do not assess the team process, then we create the very environment that draws complaints from both students and faculty regarding free riders, interpersonal conflict, and unclear direction. This is why the three aspects I have identified are so important in the team process.

All sets of individuals who are placed in a group setting must move through a series of stages to become a high-performing team. One common set of stages for group development includes forming, storming, norming, performing, and adjourning (Tuckman, 1965). For the group to move to the performance stage, the members must pass through the first three phases. Developing team core values, team purpose, and team performance management system helps the teams make this transition.

For example, defining the team's core values makes explicit what different team members think is important. It also helps define how the team will make decisions, and it establishes a set of norms for the team. Developing a

Table 7.1. Team Process Performance Standards

Percentage Achieved	Performance Standard
95–100	Significantly exceeds performance requirements and expectations
90–94	Exceeds performance requirements and expectations
70–89	Meets performance requirements and expectations
60–69	Improved performance required
1–59	Unsatisfactory performance
0	Failure to perform

team purpose—whether it is a clear, specific goal statement; a scope statement for a project; or a team mission statement—assists the team in determining what must be done to achieve the task and what product the client wants. This part of the team process helps make it clear what performance is necessary. The team performance management system defines the performance criteria that the team will use to judge the performance of each team member. In addition, it establishes how feedback will be provided to the team members regarding their performance. Finally, it establishes how the points will be allocated to each team member at the end of the project.

Even with reading materials and lectures on these three items, teams often find it difficult to produce acceptable team process materials. On the other hand, some teams have no problem producing these materials. It is impossible to determine which teams will find this an easy process and which teams will struggle with the team process. Because these materials move the individuals from being just a cluster of people to becoming a high-performance team, it is critical that the team produce at least an acceptable set of these materials. Therefore, I have built flexibility into my criterion-reference assessment.

When a team turns one of these products in, I review it. If the team process item does not reach a level that "meets performance requirements and expectations" as described in the guide, the item is returned to the team with both a grade and my comments on why the item is unacceptable. At this point, the team is given the opportunity to revise the team process item. If the revised materials reach the level that meets performance requirements and expectations, the team's grade is then adjusted. The team cannot receive the highest possible grade for revised work, but the team's grade is adjusted to the lowest end of the grading scale for the meets-performance-requirements-and-expectations standard. This flexibility in the assessment process allows my student teams to use the feedback I provide as a learning opportunity rather than a permanent negative mark on their team process.

Something that I have observed about these team process materials is that some teams just consider these items as homework assignments to be completed. They do not see that these materials are moving their team toward becoming a better team. Therefore, I require a reflection paper to be written as a team for each of these team process items. The reflection paper is to focus on why this part of the team process is important, how they will use the item they have developed, and why it is beneficial to the team. Often the initial reflection paper only describes the steps that the team took to produce the finished item and does not include reflection. I think this happens because writing a descriptive paper is safer and more familiar. Once again, the flexibility in my assessment methods allows me to provide candid and valuable feedback to the team while not sacrificing their overall grade. My experience is that this usually happens only once to a team and that they learn to adjust their behavior to produce at least acceptable materials.

Assessing the Unexpected and Serendipity

Problem-based service-learning projects by their very nature are ambiguous, messy, and unclear. Therefore, it should not surprise readers that the teams often do unexpected and serendipitous things as they try to define and ultimately resolve the problem. The problem with most traditional assessment methods is that there is no way to respond to these events. Some of these unexpected events might be categorized as positively deviant behavior. Examples are providing me with minutes from their team meetings or writing a reflection paper on some meaningful moment in their team development of which I was unaware. On the other hand, an event could be a negatively deviant behavior, such as withholding critical information from another team or acting unprofessionally with the client. These moments— whether positive or negative—should not be ignored. They are important learning moments for the team. If we do not recognize the positive behaviors, we discourage the act of producing extraordinary results. If we do this, we should expect to receive only work that minimally meets standards and nothing more. If we ignore the negative behaviors, we condone the behavior and should not be surprised if we see it repeated.

When this first happened to me, I realized immediately that I needed a way to handle these events within my assessment methods. What I developed is what I call "other activity points" (OAPs). The statement below is how this alternative assessment technique is explained in my team project manual.

Other Activity Points (OAPs)

Because teams are dynamic, it is impossible for me to know what each team will do during the learning cycle. Therefore, I have created other activity points (OAPs). These points are part of the process grade. During the learning cycle, teams will do things that I did not anticipate when I formed the teams. Some of the things will be useful in moving the team process forward or moving the task forward. Others will be detrimental to task accomplishment or inhibit team development. When I observe or experience one of these events, I will award or deduct OAPs. As you can see from the Process Worksheet, these points go into a T account. At the end of the learning cycle, I will subtract the negative point total from the positive point total. At that point, your goal should be to have at least 500 positive OAPs. If you have less than 500 points, you will be awarded whatever that value is even if it is a negative number. On the other hand, if you have more than 500 points, you will be awarded 500 points for OAPs. *Please be careful.* I have seen teams lose as many as 200 OAPs at the end of the learning cycle. Because they had not built up a significant number earlier in the learning cycle, this event seriously hurt the team's overall project score.

These points are part of the total grade for the project but are not assigned to any specific task or team process. In my classes, I have found that about 5 percent of the total points should be assigned as OAPs. I needed a way to keep track of these points, so I borrowed a technique called "T accounts" from my accounting colleagues. Exhibit 7.1 includes an example of one of these T accounts.

I keep one of these T accounts for each of my project teams. As the team does positive activities, the points and the reason for the points are placed on the left-hand side of the T account as credits. As negative events

Exhibit 7.1. An Example of a T Account of Other Activity Points

Credits		Debits	
Points	*Reason*	*Points*	*Reason*
25	Team meeting minutes 1/18/04	25	No initials on memo scheduling meeting
50	Memo scheduling meeting with advanced questions attached	50	Unprofessional behavior during practice presentation
25	Team meeting minutes 1/29/04		
75	Executive summary update on problem identification process		
25	Team meeting minutes 2/4/04		
50	Team meeting minutes 2/13/04 insightful		
100	Reflection paper on team conflict and resolution	.	
25	Team meeting minutes 2/28/04		
75	Executive summary seeking approval of new presentation format		
100	Reflection paper on after-action thoughts about the project		
Total	550	*Total*	75

Result: 550 − 75 = 475 net-awarded points.

occur, the points and the reason are placed on the right side of the T account as debits. At the end of the project, the points are summed on both sides, and the debit total is subtracted from the credit total. If there is a positive balance, those points are the ones earned by the team for OAPs. These points are added into the total project points. If the balance is negative, that number of points is subtracted from the team's project total. Although it is possible to end with negative points, no team has ever done this. Once again, the flexibility in the assessment measure allows the teams to use the feedback that comes with the assignment of the points as a learning opportunity rather than as a permanent mark against the team.

Conclusion

Problem-based service-learning projects require a flexible formative and summative assessment process. Because the project is unstructured, we should expect that the team will go down blind alleys and have some false starts. The assessment process must be designed so that we can provide the teams with feedback that is useful and also directs their behavior toward learning and adapting based on the feedback. In addition, the project is being completed for a real-world client. The students are learning not only specific content but also how to deal with a client. At times the clients may be difficult or may change their minds about what they want. In these stressful moments, students can make errors of judgment. We should not ignore these learning moments, but we should provide a way for the team to recover from this failure. We have all had moments like this in our work life, and we have been allowed to make amends and move on. Therefore, it is critical to build in a way to assess negative deviant behaviors as well as the positive deviant behaviors. From a constructivist point of view, problem-based service-learning projects allow the teams to construct their own understanding of the problem, explore that reality, obtain feedback from that exploration, and learn what to do next. Just like everyday life.

References

Anderson, R. S. "Why Talk About Different Ways to Grade? The Shift from Traditional Assessment to Alternative Assessment." In R. S. Anderson and B. W. Speck (eds.), *Changing the Way We Grade Student Performance: Classroom Assessment and the New Learning Paradigm.* New Directions for Teaching and Learning, no. 74. San Francisco: Jossey-Bass, 1998.

Barrows, H. S., and Tamblyn, R. H. *Problem-Based Learning: An Approach to Medical Education.* New York: Springer, 1980.

Cameron, K. S. "Organizational Virtuousness and Performance." In K. S. Cameron, J. E. Dutton, and R. E. Quinn (eds.), *Positive Organizational Scholarship: Foundations of a New Discipline.* San Francisco: Berrett-Koehler, 2003, pp. 48–65.

Csikszentmihalyi, M. *Good Business: Leadership, Flow, and the Making of Meaning.* New York: Viking, 2003.

Hellriegel, D., and Slocum, J. W., Jr. *Organizational Behavior.* (10th ed.) Mason, Ohio: South-Western College Publishing, 2004.

McCarthy, A., and Tucker, M. "Student Attitudes Toward Service Learning: Implications for Implementation." *Journal of Management Education,* 1999, 23(5), 554–573.

Peterson, T. O. "So You're Thinking of Trying Problem-Based Learning? Three Critical Success Factors for Implementation." *Journal of Management Education,* forthcoming.

Smith, K. A. "Cooperative Learning: Making 'Groupwork' Work." In T. E. Sutherlund and C. C. Bonwell (eds.), *Using Active Learning in College Classes: A Range of Options for Faculty.* New Directions for Teaching and Learning, no. 67. San Francisco: Jossey-Bass, 1996.

Smith, K. A. "Grading Cooperative Projects." In R. S. Anderson and B. W. Speck (eds.), *Changing the Way We Grade Student Performance: Classroom Assessment and the New Learning Paradigm.* New Directions for Teaching and Learning, no. 74. San Francisco: Jossey-Bass, 1998.

Tuckman, B. "Developmental Sequence in Small Groups." *Psychological Bulletin,* 1965, 63, 384–399.

TIM O. PETERSON *is professor of management at Oklahoma State University.*

*Whether in the science or language laboratory, carrying
out health care procedures or demonstrating performance
arts, faculty can improve skill evaluation through
transparency and authenticity in exam construction,
format, and grading.*

Performance-Based Assessment: Improving the Value of Laboratory and Skills Examinations

Judy M. Silvestrone

Assess it, and it becomes important. Assess it explicitly . . . with
transparent criteria, and perhaps they will see why.
—James, 2000, p. 355

Enhancing the quality of examinations is always a creditable goal. Improving skill assessment presents unique challenges because of the nature of the evaluation and the traditions of various disciplines. In this chapter, I address how choices in the construction and grading of practical examinations can improve transparency (explicitness) and authenticity (relation to real tasks) and thereby increase the capacity to examine the most essential skill sets.

Transparency in examination refers to the explicit definition and communication of guidelines for evaluation (James, 2000; Moskal, 2003; Simon and Forgette-Giroux, 2001). Whereas this is consciously and consistently prepared for cognitive assessment in most courses, there are subtleties to skill examination that warrant special attention. In particular, skill assessment benefits from the development of specialized learning objectives, the elucidation of performance expectations, and the separation of cognitive from skills evaluation.

Authenticity refers to the use of acquired knowledge in relationship to other courses, ideas, and real-world tasks. Validity and reliability in any examination are improved by presenting real-world challenges (Wiggins, 1990). Skill examination benefits by the selection of the appropriate form of evidence, delineation of the weight of various elements, and the identification of variables that can decrease validity. In the ensuing discussion, I examine means for maximizing transparency and authenticity in learning objectives, assessment construction, and grading.

Learning Objectives

One of the simplest methods faculty can use to ensure the quality of skill evaluation is to construct and communicate explicit learning objectives for each skill set. Although cognitive objectives are typically included in course syllabi, psychomotor and affective objectives may not be as well developed or expressly conveyed to students. Psychomotor objectives include specific performance criteria such as speed, dexterity, strength, and functional expectations. Affective learning objectives can include attitude and communication. For instance, in a nursing program, it would be appropriate to include both proper venipuncture technique (psychomotor) and appropriate patient concern (affective) as valued learning objectives. These objectives are vital to the future application of the skill and deserve appropriate consideration and assessment.

Examination Construction

There are several issues to consider with regard to the construction of examinations in courses using performance-based assessment.

Cognition Versus Performance. When constructing an examination, faculty should consider separating cognitive tasks from performance unless they are inextricably linked. Different understanding is demonstrated through action than through written examination. For assessment in the Spanish language laboratory, James (2000) indicates that disaggregation of performance helps students see the importance of individual skills and increases their transferability to other venues.

An instructor might consider offering a separate cognitive exam or provide a reading period before the examination for students to prepare responses necessary during the skill evaluation. In medicine, Wilkerson and Lee state that "knowing *how* to perform the physical examination and knowing *when* to perform it may be very different skills" (Wilkerson and Lee, 2003, p. S31, emphasis added).

Context of the Test. Context, however, remains important in the relevance of the skills to be learned, the manner in which they will be applied in future endeavors, and the realism of the conditions in which students are examined. Scrutinizing the expected application of the skill allows the suitability of both the objective and method of assessment to be determined. For example, does sight-reading have a convincing rationale as part of a performance evaluation when music students would otherwise realistically have rehearsal time before recital? The answer may be that sight-reading *is* a crucial requirement, but the decision to use it must be made consciously and with the targeted application in mind. The reasons for conditions imposed on performance should be made explicit to students so that the relevance of the limitations are evident, rather than appearing arbitrary.

Appropriate Evidence. Moskal and Leydens (2000) indicate that reflection on the learning objectives and purpose of the assessment will make apparent the best forms of evidence for identifying these skills. Examination of the method should prompt the question: "Does this method truly reveal competency in the skill sets I want to examine?" For example, is there a strong rationale for examining students in an anatomy lab by having them rotate through thirty one-minute stations in which they identify tagged structures? What would be more typical of the real-life demands of a paleontologist or a physician? Will such a rapid pace ever really be essential? In real life, what is more critical, accuracy or speed?

For evidence of student development over time, teachers in many disciplines use portfolios of accumulated work accompanied by a self-reflection on progress and process. The use of videotaped skill performance over time with student self-assessment can provide a profound learning experience for the student and good evidence of development of the skill.

Overcoming Measurement Obstacles in Performance Testing

Obstacles that limit accuracy of skill assessment include situations that require transfer before the student is ready, time constraints, and performance anxiety.

Too Far a Transfer Required. Although transferability of skill is a goal of instruction, an examination should not be the first time that a student is asked to use a skill in a new manner or for a new situation. Students should get the opportunity to rehearse using skills in various circumstances; explore connections between cognitive and skill sets; and practice using the critical thinking, synthesis, or problem solving expected of them before being asked to do so for evaluative purposes.

Not Enough Time Allowed. Another pertinent question is whether the use of time constraints in performance assessment is necessary. Such constraints are more frequently found in performance tests, which must be administered to a series of students in a short time or which involve several students needing access to equipment sequentially, as in a lab stations format. Temporal limits may be required because of class time but can just as often be based on faculty convenience or disciplinary tradition. There may be alternative forms of evaluation that allow for a more accurate assessment of the skill set. Can the same behaviors be assessed by a less complex procedure or with a checklist rather than a full-blown demonstration? For example, is it really necessary for a student to work all problems completely if demonstrating how to set up the problem correctly would 90 percent of the time result in a correct computation? Can time on assessment be saved by targeting the key points rather than requiring a full demonstration each time?

The use of other class sessions (such as recitation sessions) or open lab hours to allow more examination time could be considered, as well as the accumulation of quiz opportunities rather than one-shot tests to assess student progress and retention over time. Discussion with colleagues, teaching assistants, and student focus groups (such as small-group instructional diagnosis) may result in some innovative methods for performance assessment that will not be hampered by time constraints.

For some settings—food preparation, emergency procedures, or simultaneous translation—performance under time constraints may be crucial. A common recommendation for those instances is to allow one-and-a-half greater time than required by a graduate student for adequate performance of the same assessment (Smee, 2003). However, it has been my experience that when an exam is constructed well (and externally reviewed), most students do not need the full time that was initially allotted. When the urgency of time is eliminated, students perform better and often faster. When a student's progress through a performance test is affected by the progress of others (such as in moving from one lab station to the next), credit can be given for timely completion or for partial completion to encourage students not to linger over a single station.

If time *is* essential, removing disruptive prompts to indicate time passing (such as a bell, buzzer, or timer) may improve accurateness of evaluation. Having a human voice prompt to "move to the next station or question" provokes less anxiety. When multistation examinations are necessary, use a "revisit" period at the end of the examination when students can check back on a few stations. Unnecessary transit time and time spent orienting to a specimen or problem can be reduced by decreasing the number of stations or problems and asking multiple questions at each. Wilkerson and Lee (2003) recommend that if time constraints are an essential component of the skill, time management should also be part of instruction and practice for that skill. The bottom line has never been more accurately summarized than by a question raised by one professor: "Do we want our students to know it better or faster?"

Coping with Performance Anxiety. Whatever assessment type is chosen, sharing the details of the format, conditions, and process of the examination with students improves exam quality. Skill assessment inherently carries with it the increased risk for test anxiety (a form of performance anxiety) due to the requirements of demonstration and observation.

For an assessment of what students know to be fair and accurate, with minimal influence by performance anxiety or lack of familiarity with exam format, students need to be apprised of precise expectations. Sharing objectives, test system, and grading criteria with students early in the course is vital to decrease their anxiety with novel exam formats (Moskal, 2003;

McGregor and Elliott, 2002). Simulated examinations for practice can provide grading opportunities, frequent feedback on performance, and familiarity with exam schema. There are special concerns when videotaping or audiorecording students' performance. If they are used only in the testing environment, students may view their purpose as potentially punitive or threatening. The purpose of recording should be made explicit, previously modeled, and best used for self-assessment.

Grading the Performance

In the grading process, an explanation of the weight of various elements, attention to level of detail, and distribution of sample grading forms and graded work can support a quality assessment and reduce grading challenges.

What Is Included? Performance can be graded on the use of process, the final product, or a combination of both. The relative value and effect of these elements should be delineated (Moskal and Leydens, 2000; Woods and others, 2001). Just as in a cognitive problem in mathematics, students should be aware what weight is assigned to the reasoning or construct behind the performance and the resultant outcome. For example, in a musical recital, what is the expected weight of technical performance versus emotive factors? Transparency of partial credit policies also serves to decrease perceived variance and subjectivity in grading.

What Level of Detail Is Expected? Explicit grading criteria, weight, and level of detail help students understand expectations (Silvestrone, 2002). Students should be aware of the value assigned to different aspects of their performance. Some errors or omissions may have relatively little weight, but others may prompt inevitable failure or retake. A radiological technologist might fail an examination by taking the wrong x-ray image on a patient (or simulation) but not for using the incorrect film size. For a comparative anatomy examination, if a student has identified a groove on a bone, does he or she also need to name that bone? Is the identification required in English or Latin nomenclature? Examples of expected work (such as vocabulary lists) may help students identify the level of detail necessary. Including these lists in the syllabus or before the examination gives students a necessary frame of reference for the depth and orientation of their response or performance.

Value of a Good Model. Furthermore, there is a strong foundation for providing graded examples to students. Seeing examples of student work and the reasons for the grade assignments communicates standards to new students and lecturers (James, 2000; Simon and Forgette-Giroux, 2001). Even more benefit can be derived if students see multiple examples or are allowed to participate in the evaluation of an example. When students see how the criteria are being applied, they get a clearer idea of how to prepare their own responses to an exam.

Inter-Rater Reliability. Idiosyncratic grading can be an issue with performances being evaluated by multiple raters or multiple sections (Baughin, Brod, and Page, 2002; Smee, 2003). To increase inter-rater and intrarater reliability, the use of primary trait analysis (grading rubric or matrix) is optimal (Simon and Forgette-Giroux, 2001; Chapter Twelve of this volume). With a substantial history in primary and secondary education, rubrics have special value for performance-based examination in higher education courses and programs. Rubrics can decrease grade variance with multiple raters, multiple assessments, and student progress over time. Teaching assistants and lead faculty can work together to construct rubrics with up to five levels of accomplishment over a broad number of evaluation areas. James (2000) recommends the use of rubrics in the language laboratory to allow evaluation of technical skills as well as language. Rubrics allow for a single rater to evaluate key skill components with the stroke of a pen or the touch of a palm-held computer screen.

An additional benefit of rubrics is that grade challenges are decreased when students have the opportunity to see the evaluative criteria and attendant grade levels in advance (Moskal and Leydens, 2000). Students use these criteria for exam preparation, monitoring their content coverage, and self-feedback.

Many authors espouse the use of a three-tiered rubric, with expected characteristics, behaviors, or skill proficiency delineated for each level. Such ratings as "good, pass, not ready" or "meets expectations, exceeds expectations, does not meet expectations" with descriptors provide sound feedback for students and support consistency in grading. Instructions for their construction and sample rubrics may be found in Walvoord and Johnson's (1998) *Effective Grading,* or on Web sites such as http://www.rubistar.4teachers.org or http://www.teach-nology.com/web_tools/rubrics. Many disciplines have rubrics already constructed in light of the outcomes-based assessment movement affecting certification by professional associations.

Conclusion

Increasing authenticity and transparency of learning objectives and grading criteria does not entail decreasing intellectual challenge or integrity of skill assessment. The quality of an examination increases when learning objectives are constructed in depth, clearly communicated, and applied throughout examination administration and grading. Both students and faculty benefit when this communication is coupled with strategies for reducing variables that decrease validity and relevance of the skills and assessment to the larger world.

Moskal (2003) states the goals of skill assessment nicely when discussing the use of rubrics in engineering: "Performance assessments require more time to administer than do other forms of assessment. The investment of this classroom time should result in a higher payoff. This payoff should include both an increase in the teacher's understanding of what students know and can do and an increase in the students' knowledge of the intended content and constructs" (p. 2).

References

Baughin, J. A., Brod, E. F., and Page, D. L. "Primary Trait Analysis: A Tool for Classroom-Based Assessment." *College Teaching*, 2002, *50*(2), 75–80.

James, P. "A Blueprint for Skills Assessment in Higher Education." *Assessment and Evaluation in Higher Education*, 2000, *25*(4), 353–367.

McGregor, H. A., and Elliott, A. J. "Achievement Goals as Predictors of Achievement-Relevant Processes Prior to Task Engagement." *Journal of Educational Psychology*, 2002, *94*(2), 381–391.

Moskal, B. M. "Recommendations for Developing Classroom Performance Assessments and Scoring Rubrics." *Practical Assessment, Research, and Evaluation*, 2003, *8*(14). Retrieved Nov. 15, 2004, from http://PAREonline.net/getvn.asp?v=8&n=14.

Moskal, B. M., and Leydens, J. A. "Scoring Rubric Development: Validity and Reliability." *Practical Assessment, Research, and Evaluation*, 2000, *7*(10). Retrieved Nov. 15, 2004, from http://PAREonline.net/getvn.asp?v=7&n=10.

Silvestrone, J. M. "Better Exam Content and Format Lift Value of Evaluation." *Teaching Professor*, 2002, *16*(8), 1, 3.

Simon, M., and Forgette-Giroux, R. "A Rubric for Scoring Postsecondary Academic Skills." *Practical Assessment, Research, and Evaluation*, 2001, *7*(18). Retrieved Nov. 15, 2004, from http://PAREonline.net/getvn.asp?v=7&n=18.

Smee, S. "ABC of Learning and Teaching in Medicine: Skill Based Assessment." *British Medical Journal*, 2003, *326*(7391), 703–706.

Walvoord, B. E., and Johnson, V. A. *Effective Grading: A Tool for Learning and Assessment*. San Francisco: Jossey-Bass, 1998.

Wiggins, G. *The Case for Authentic Assessment*. Washington, D.C.: ERIC Clearinghouse on Tests Measurement and Evaluation, 1990. (ED 328 611)

Wilkerson, L., and Lee, M. "Assessing Physical Examination Skills of Senior Medical Students: Knowing How Versus Knowing When." *Academic Medicine*, 2003, *78*(10), S30–S32.

Woods, D. R., and others. "Assessing Problem-Solving Skills. Part I: The Context for Assessment." *Chemical Engineering Education*, Fall 2001, 300–307.

JUDY M. SILVESTRONE *is professor of clinical sciences at New York Chiropractic College and director of the Center for Academic Support.*

PART THREE

Influence of Technology on Assessment Possibilities

Although instructional methods are moving in ever greater number to a multimedia base, testing is not. What principles should be considered in correcting this misalignment?

Aligning Paper Tests with Multimedia Instruction

Scott L. Howell

Although the "click-and-point" virtual classrooms of today hardly resemble the brick-and-mortar classrooms of yesterday, one thing seems not to have changed: the prevalence of paper-based tests. Paper-based tests have been the staple of education for centuries and will most likely persist for many years to come. This article explores some of the issues surrounding the growing chasm between the way students are now taught and how they are still tested from three perspectives: researcher, student, and teacher.

Should educators be concerned with the widening gap in how teachers teach, using rich multimedia in a multidimensional context, and how teachers test, on paper in grayscale colors in a two-dimensional setting? Should a new generation of students who communicate, learn, and almost live on keyboards be subjected to paper-based tests that require them to use less familiar handwriting tools, such as pens and number two lead pencils in an unfamiliar context—not on the computer? I believe educators should be concerned with the lag that prevails in aligning and changing assessment practices to the changed, and changing, instructional practices that now depend so much on computer-based multimedia environments.

Reliability and Validity

In assessment parlance, two words prevail in almost every discussion and analysis: reliability and validity. A test's reliability is a measure of how consistent the test measures each time administered, and its validity is a measure of accuracy in representing the intent or construct of the test instrument.

A casual dart game at home where the goal is to see who can get the most darts closest to the bull's-eye may be illustrative of these rather abstract concepts of reliability and validity and helpful in our discussion about paper tests in a computer-based instructional context. The proximity of the darts to the bull's-eye is the goal of the game or the "construct." The participant who successfully clusters the darts tightly will have high reliability or consistency; the participant who not only clusters the darts but does so nearest to, or even on, the bull's-eye is also the most accurate or valid. A test or a dart game can have high reliability with low validity, but one with high validity will also have high reliability.

Whether in dart play or test taking, all participants expect—independent of high, average, or low scores—reliable and valid scores that predict within some acceptable range of variability the appropriate level of mastery. However, the stakes are much higher in test taking than in dart playing, especially with their legal implications, when the measurements from these tests determine either directly or indirectly placement, college admission, and even employment.

Just as a dart player anticipates after weeks of practicing to see the same kind of dartboard at the "big" contest, so does the student in either a physical or virtual classroom studying a subject expect to see the same kind of subject matter presentation on the exam. If at the casual dart contest the darts are made of lighter or heavier material, the board resized, and the bull's-eye situated in the corner rather than the center as found previously, would anyone predict the results or measurements to be either reliable or valid on the day of the contest?

Much like the dart game is advancing to the electronic age with its new darts and electronically sensitized boards, so is the instructional experience changing from using only pencils, pens, and blackboards to the ubiquitous use of keyboards, computer screens, and software applications. Everyone would agree that practicing the dart game the "new" way but then showing up at a contest where the game was played the "old" way just would not be fair, but is this not exactly what is happening in many of our classrooms (physical and virtual) as students taught one way take tests another way?

What Are the Issues?

What are some of the issues with teaching online and testing on paper from the perspectives of a researcher, a student, and a teacher?

Researcher Perspective. This specific question of comparability between paper- and computer-based test results—assuming rich, multimedia instruction—has not been thoroughly studied. Not only are there few studies on this topic extant, but it is expected that there will never be many in the future because of research methods concerns and the commonsensical need for alignment between teaching and testing methods. Most researchers hesitate to conduct this comparison study because of well-founded criticism that has mounted over media comparison studies in recent years, especially in the field of education. One of the most compelling reasons either for not researching this comparison or for discrediting the results of any comparability studies conducted is the difficulty of randomly selecting student participants in control and treatment groups, especially with all of the practical and ethical concerns associated with inaccurate test results. Nonetheless, one practical researcher has suggested that this issue still merits evaluation. Frederick (2003) has said that "as the environment changes for the delivery of instruction, it is important to reevaluate the ways in which we assess the learning outcome for students using this new format and develop and apply assessment techniques that are more consistent with the learning environment" (p. 17).

Student Perspective. The students of today are technologically savvy and sophisticated; they also are not patient with what they call old-fashioned teaching or testing practices. Students are accustomed to keyboarding as they communicate with friends using e-mail and instant text messaging; a toggle stick is a mere extension of their hand, and they have developed motor skills to prove it in computer game competitions with self and others; and most students have access to a computer either at home or at school where many of them learn, play, and do their homework. At the time of this writing, I attended a junior high awards ceremony, and the assistant principal mentioned as an aside that the ninth-grade student who was receiving an outstanding academic award also keyboarded at a rate of 130 words per minute.

As accustomed as today's students are to keyboards, toggle sticks, and computers, they are also as unaccustomed to using number two pencils to fill in test bubble sheets using optical character recognition technology and pens of yesteryear to write long (or even short) papers and essays. Although many students have refined the motor skills of "click, point, and drag" with a mouse, keyboard, or toggle stick and can experience little fatigue doing so, it does not take long for cramps, physical fatigue, and psychological discomfort to impair a student who is unaccustomed to writing by hand for extended periods of time with pencils and pens. Two researchers from Boston College have concluded that "recent research shows that written tests taken on paper severely underestimate the performance of students accustomed to working on computers. The situation is analogous to testing the accounting skills of modern accountants, but restricting them to the use of an abacus for calculations" (Russell and Haney, 2000, p. 2).

Teacher Perspective. Even though teachers may be involved as much as a fourth of their time doing some form of assessment, most have never received formal instruction on good test-writing practices. Training in such practices would help teachers improve their tests, but even then, little of the training would emphasize the need to incorporate the same multimedia used throughout the course in their tests. Furthermore, tests are often the one neglected part of the instruction process because developing good tests (and even poor tests) is a difficult and time-consuming process.

In recent years, school administrators have told teachers that they will "jump aboard" in the classroom (physical or virtual) with any of a number of technological initiatives that have swept their schools, districts, and universities. Many publishers have packaged textbooks and instructors' manuals with CD-ROMS, videos, and supporting Web sites to help "sell" the textbooks and enrich the instruction; yet, the exam banks and tests stay the same two-dimensional, static, grayscale items that they have always been. Some teachers have embraced these new technological and instructional methods willingly and have even taught themselves new skills necessary to keep up with—not ahead of—their own students' technological expectations; other teachers would if they could but lack the necessary training, support, and time necessary to acquire new skills; and still others refuse to abandon the habits and practices of many years of instruction, knowing that retirement cannot be far away. The unevenness that exists among the teachers in this regard also exists in different regions of the country for a complexity of reasons, from cultural to economic to political to others.

Even though there may not be parity across teachers' integration of technology, multimedia, animation, simulation, color, audio, and video into the curriculum, there is no question that this integration into instruction has occurred in the classrooms of today much more quickly than has the integration of the same into assessment. That this alignment between how teachers teach and how they test needs to occur is clear. What is not as clear is what the barriers are to change and how best to remove them!

Conclusion

Whereas the multimedia-enhanced instruction and the virtual classrooms of today no longer resemble the classrooms of even ten years ago, regrettably, the one instructional element that has stayed the same is the tests. Chalkboards have given way to computer projection screens, keyboarding has replaced handwriting, and multimedia simulations and animations now enhance many learning activities, but still tests are categorically unchanged in their paper-based format.

I suggest that the very pillars and fundamentals of sound test construction and delivery—reliability and validity—are threatened by this misalignment between teaching and testing methods. Researchers, students, and instructors alike agree, although from different perspectives, that urgent changes are needed to update and align the antiquated paper-based tests of the past to the rich multimedia- and computer-based teaching environments of today and tomorrow.

References

Frederick, P. "The Need for Alternative Authentic Assessments in Online Learning Environments." *Journal of Instruction Delivery Systems,* 2003, 16(1), 17–20.

Russell, M., and Haney, W. "Bridging the Gap Between Testing and Technology in Schools." *Education Policy Analysis,* 2000, 8(19). Retrieved June 7, 2004, from http://epaa.asu.edu/epaa/v8n19.html.

SCOTT L. HOWELL is adjunct professor of instructional psychology and technology at Brigham Young University in Provo, Utah.

10

Can computers help with one of the most persistent challenges of large classes: the accurate and efficient measurement of student learning?

Computerized Testing in Large Courses: A Case Study

John F. Kremer

This case study is about a highly enrolled introductory psychology course at a large (twenty-eight thousand students) research-oriented urban university. This course was taught in large lecture halls. Students' grades were determined solely by their performance on multiple-choice tests. The "DWF rate" (those who did not pass the course) was consistently around 40 percent. More than ten years ago, we started with the hypothesis that this rate could be reduced and that these students could learn to succeed. The first step in this process was to institute computerized testing. Annually, the Psychology Testing Lab assesses over four thousand students. The lab is a four-hundred-square-foot room that originally supported sixteen computers. Students take five tests per semester, and they are permitted to take each test twice. Initially, when tests closed on the weekend, students often waited in long lines. The focus of this chapter will be on the lessons that we have learned in implementing computerized testing with limited resources.

Lessons Learned

Computerized testing in large courses provides flexibility for students and faculty as well as solving some space problems. However, test security issues can continue to be a challenge. In the final analysis, computerized testing encourages course development and coherence.

Flexibility of Computerized Testing Provides Numerous Advantages for Students and Faculty. Students may take tests almost any time of the day and any day of the week. Our urban students have myriad other life responsibilities. For example, students spend more time working (twenty-two hours per week) than attending class (eighteen hours per week) or studying outside class (fifteen hours per week). They appreciate the ability to plan their tests around their other academic and life tasks. Flexibility also helps faculty. Faculty members can open and close the tests at their discretion and can easily extend the test for individual students. The ease of providing students with a makeup test has enabled faculty to be more responsive to the unexpected demands in students' lives.

Space and Other Problems Can Be Solved. Administering well over ten thousand tests per semester in a four-hundred-square-foot room with sixteen computers was a daunting task. We had long lines, complaints about noise, and actually a fight or two. Problem solving gradually reduced these problems, and the lab today has few lines and complaints. Several strategies pushed this progress:

The test closing dates for individual sections are staggered based on enrollment.

Students are required to wait twelve hours before taking tests again.

On a "Testing Reservation" home page, students can find the times when the lab is busy and reserve one of the testing computers.

If a line occurs, students are given a return time, and a computer is reserved for them.

The lab was also redesigned with smaller compact computers and screens to reduce crowding and yet increase the number of computers by 40 percent.

An additional problem was the amount of noise caused by the number of people in the small lab, noisy keyboards and computers, and student-proctor conversations. Changing to soundless keyboards and quieter computer fans, adding carpet, and providing more space between students reduced the noise. Students may also use earphones and listen to repeating sounds or melodies that mask the noise in the room and from the hall outside. To reduce student-proctor conversations, students sign into the lab on a keyboard mounted to the open door of the lab, and the computer gives directions and assigns students to a testing space.

Test Security Issues Are a Persistent Challenge. Initially, the lab was designed to be low maintenance: Students would simply go into the lab and take their tests with only sporadic and random supervision. However, students soon complained about the high amount of student dishonesty. Over the years, types of academic misconduct included unauthorized written notes, unauthorized notes on the computer screen, conversations with other students, hacking into the test bank, printing off the tests, and taking the test for other students. A variety of strategies were used to counteract these problems. The following steps were instituted to reduce the probability of similar items appearing on adjacent computer screens:

- Each test has five versions of nonoverlapping items
- The items for each test are randomly presented to students, and no student gets the same test twice
- Test items are randomly presented one at a time
- Work-study students are used as testing proctors
- Work-study students are trained, supervised, and monitored
- Proctors are able to easily observe student screens after the room was rearranged, the proctor's station was elevated, and proctors were given a computer program to directly observe each student's computer screen
- Video cameras were strategically placed in the lab
- Printing was disabled from any of the computer terminals
- A computer programmer effectively secured the test items from hackers
- To prevent one student from taking the test for another student, proctors check the students' identification cards
- Students swipe their identification card to gain access to the test; the test then is available only to the student who is identified on the card
- To prevent many different types of academic misconduct, students may hit a button on the computer screen to report cheating to a proctor in the lab
- Before taking the test, students must read a code-of-conduct statement and agree to abide by the principles in the statement; this promise includes the responsibility to report incidents of academic misconduct when they occur

By having a central testing location, most of the unethical behaviors that occur not only in the lab but also in a typical classroom are eliminated or reduced. Computerized testing presents unique unethical possibilities, but these are easily identified and reduced by careful problem solving.

Computerized Testing Encourages Course Development and Coherence. Centralizing the testing function of a large course frees up resources to develop not only the administration of the test (items noted above) but also the content of the test and other course components. The following strategies helped integrate the many components of the course into a more cohesive package.

Different Types of Test Items and Item Responses Were Added to Better Measure Course Objectives. After initial programming, one of the principal advantages of computer assessment is the ability to easily combine several different methods of assessment. One of the objectives for this course was to help students apply psychological concepts and theories to real-life examples. So test items include not only written applications but also audio-visual items from existing movies or acted scripts that were taped for the test. On the response side, the tests combine traditional multiple-choice answers and short-essay questions. To reduce faculty time in scoring the twenty-five thousand essays, student raters grade the essays using scoring criteria and sample essays to enhance reliability. Raters have access to the essays from any Web site and typically grade the essays within twenty-four hours. However, with this volume of work, raters are not able to provide adequate feedback. A computerized essay content grader will soon be used to not only grade essays but also give feedback to students.

Content Validity of the Test Was Improved. Because the same five tests are used across forty sections of this course, a significant amount of time and attention is given to the development of items. For example, this course has five critical thinking goals based on Bloom's (1956) taxonomy. Each chapter has a grid with about one hundred fifty cells (thirty concepts, names, or theories by five critical thinking skills). The cells of the grid are used to develop test questions and items for the computer exercises and written homework. The grid is also available to students and faculty to help them prepare for tests and plan class activities.

Focus of Computerized Activities Was Expanded to Include Not Only Evaluative (Summative) Assessment but Also Developmental (Formative) Assessment. When the tests were working both administratively and conceptually, resources were directed toward developing homework assignments and computer exercises to help students learn the material and give them developmental feedback when they need it and based on their performance. Separate exercises focused on each of the critical thinking goals of the course, and other exercises helped students put it all together and review for the tests.

Summary and Conclusion

I hope that this chapter makes a case for using computerized testing in large courses by pointing out the following advantages: Multiple sources of assessment can be easily integrated, audiovisual items and multiple-response formats can be used to measure higher-order thinking skills (application, analysis, and synthesis), students' educational needs can determine the timing and type of feedback, instructors can easily assess students' progress toward their learning goals, variability in assessment across instructors and raters is reduced, and assessment goals can be integrated into all aspects of the course. On the other hand, computerized testing does come with its share of hassles (too little space, crowded conditions, new test security issues). An increase in the use of technology creates questions and needs that professors are not accustomed to answering. By combining sections and courses and reorganizing resources, departments and schools can engage in strategic planning to meet these needs. The use of computerized testing and other efficient uses of technology can provide better services to students while decreasing the load on instructors and making a better use of physical resources. However, departments or schools must make a commitment to stay abreast of the newest developments in technology to improve and to even maintain a computerized testing program.

Reference

Bloom, B. S. (ed.). *Taxonomy of Educational Objectives: The Classification of Educational Goals. Handbook 1: Cognitive Domain.* New York: McKay, 1956.

JOHN F. KREMER *is professor of psychology at Indiana University–Purdue University Indianapolis.*

PART FOUR

Moving Beyond the Individual to Group Tests

11

Group exams in science courses can enhance students' achievement and encourage retention of students within the discipline. The challenge to instructors is to recognize when and how they are best used.

Group Exams in Science Courses

Linda C. Hodges

Using group exams in science courses is an appealing idea to some instructors and an oxymoron to others. On the positive side, this form of testing may allow instructors to pose more challenging questions, relying on the power of peer learning to help more students move ahead in their understanding of complex ideas. The downside, however, is that it poses particular challenges to instructors in terms of ascertaining if individual students are advancing in their learning and in finding an appropriate balance between individual accountability and group dependence. For students, group exams may provide needed support and incentives as they struggle with the abstract and sometimes overwhelming content in science classes. But some students may resent this format, fearing that their less-motivated peers benefit from the hard work of others. In this chapter, I discuss some of the advantages to this form of assessment and some of the caveats.

Why Use Group Exams in Science Classes?

Working together in groups on exams capitalizes on the advantages of peer learning and cooperative or collaborative learning in general. Specifically, students must articulate ideas verbally, which requires that they construct logical responses to questions based on their understanding that they then must defend to their peers. This activity may help students develop a more critical stance toward scientific knowledge and help them advance beyond a right-or-wrong approach to ideas (Nelson, 1999). This approach correlates with the constructivist model of how people learn and, intriguingly, may have an underlying physiological basis in how the brain moves information from short-term to long-term memory, as discussed by Zull (2002). At least one study supports the idea that students retain knowledge longer when examined on that information in a collaborative testing format (Cortright, Collins, Rodenbaugh, and DiCarlo, 2003).

Research in cognitive science has documented the importance of prior knowledge and experience in affecting new learning. Students often come into science classes with naïve explanations of natural phenomena that pose real impediments to their developing a more sophisticated understanding. These misconceptions can be particularly resistant to change, often persisting if addressed solely in a traditional lecture format. These alternate conceptions may be confronted explicitly when disagreements arise in group testing situations and may either be corrected by better-informed peers or may provide feedback to the instructor on underlying obstructions to learning.

Group exams allow instructors to pose more challenging questions on exams, ones that require students to analyze data, choose between alternate interpretations, explain complex phenomena, and design experiments. The ability of individual members of the group to add their particular expertise to addressing a more difficult problem can enhance students' self-confidence and promote their ability to see themselves as able to do science, important motivating factors for students' persistence in the discipline (Tobias, 1994; Seymour and Hewitt, 1997).

Finally, some research suggests that for certain students, making the science classroom a more collaborative, rather than competitive, environment increases students' motivation and enjoyment of the subject, resulting in increased retention rates in those courses. Given the diversity of the college student population today, providing diverse approaches to assessment may help instructors get a more accurate view of both how and how well their students are learning.

When to Use Group Exams Versus Other Assessments

Given the possible reasons why instructors might use group exams in science courses, when are they a most appropriate choice for assessing learning? First, group exams are probably a most meaningful assessment when other aspects of the course include a collaborative or group component. The social challenges of group decision making mean that students need some practice in navigating the group culture before being put to the test, literally and figuratively speaking. If working in groups effectively is one of the goals of a class, then group exams serve to validate this aspect of the course.

If students are familiar with the group-learning format, then group exams are appropriate for posing higher-order thinking questions (analysis, synthesis, and evaluation of data, for example) because support for the challenge is provided through peer learning. The discussion of complex concepts within the group can help students deepen their understanding by exploring how their new ideas fit within what they already know and comparing that with the perception and interpretation of others. Some instructors note that the exam under these conditions becomes a learning experience itself in addition to an assessment (Tobias and Raphael, 1997a, 1997b; Ochoa and others, 2004; Chapter Thirteen in this issue).

Finally, the group exam format can ease the anxiety faced by students who may feel less comfortable with what they perceive to be the competitive nature of the individual exam. The success they experience in the group setting can buoy their confidence and help motivate them to improve their performance on individual assessments. If student achievement, motivation, and retention in the course are particular challenges in science classes, instructors may find group exams an effective way to address these issues constructively.

How to Use Group Exams: Examples of Formats

Examples from instructors in biology, chemistry, geology, and physics classes include the use of group exams as part of an array of assessments in both introductory and upper-level classes (Tobias and Raphael, 1997a, 1997b). Instructors have used group exams in a variety of formats and settings: as stand-alone assessments, as part of an individual exam, as a follow-up to an identical individual exam, or as part of a laboratory assessment. Each of these versions are described below.

Group Exams as Stand-Alone Assessments. Particularly in situations where the learning has been done in a group format, the group exam can be the sole assessment method in a course. Some have claimed that to do so would encourage too much dependence on others. An interesting way to encourage individual accountability is to alternate between individual and group quizzes without announcing the format ahead of time.

Group Exams as Part of an Individual Exam. A common use of group exams is in a hybrid format with an individual exam. Students take an individual exam, and then one or more questions are given to them in groups. The group portion can be during the same testing period or at a separate time. Instructors report counting the group portion of the exam in a range from 20 to 50 percent of the overall exam grade.

A variation of this format involves students answering a particularly challenging question on the exam first as an individual and then again in groups. In this version, students take and turn in the whole exam as an individual, and then some part of that exam is taken in groups. The individual exam counts for some portion of the grade (75 percent is a common number), and the remainder of the grade is determined by the group response to the question, with all members of the group receiving the same score on that part.

Group Exams as a Follow-Up to an Individual Exam. Structured cooperative learning formats commonly use group exams after students take the identical exam as individuals. Frequently the group grade is higher, reinforcing the benefit of group work (Millis and Cottell, 1998). Team-based learning uses group exams in this way as part of the readiness assurance process (Michaelson, Knight, and Fink, 2002). Instructors may add the individual and group scores or use the group scores in some proportion as a bonus. This dual-exam approach has the benefit of including both individual accountability and positive interdependence in the assessment, two factors critical for the success of cooperative learning.

Group Assessments of Laboratories. Laboratory portions of courses often involve students working in groups and provide a fairly easy setting to incorporate group tests. Instructors report using group exams to test pre-lab preparation, to debrief after a particular lab session, to pose challenging lab exercises, or to probe students' understanding in an oral forum in lieu of written lab reports (Tobias and Raphael, 1997a, 1997b).

Peer Coaching During Individual Exams. Instructors who do not feel comfortable using group exams per se to evaluate students may appreciate the idea of peer coaching during individual exams. Examples of this include taking a set amount of time during an individual exam to allow study groups to talk together about the exam (with or without their exam papers). Or students may take individual exams, have an interval for group discussion, and then retake their exams again individually. In the latter case, the two scores may be averaged, or the scores after discussion may be linked to bonus points, perhaps weighted to reflect the amount of improvement across the group. For example, if individual scores increase overall by twenty points, each student may receive a proportion, say 10 percent, of those total extra points. This practice encourages students to teach each other because the more the overall point scores increase, the more bonus points everyone receives.

Caveats, Challenges, and Choices

For anyone who has made a foray into group work in general and group exams in particular, the challenges are clear: students who freeload off others, students who resent the format for that or other reasons, students who have good ideas but cave in to students who are more verbally forceful or persuasive, students who reinforce other students' misconceptions, and faculty's discomfort in mediating group dynamics. Some may even worry about potential legal issues associated with assigning one grade to a group without any individual accountability. For these reasons, many instructors report using some kind of compromise approach that ensures that students are never penalized because of poor performance or "social loafing" by some member of the group.

In general, student achievement is improved by using group exams, and often students come to realize and appreciate this aspect of the course format. The challenge remains, however, that not all students work equally well in groups, and faculty may feel poorly prepared to help students develop necessary social skills. Most instructors cite this as a fairly rare problem, however, and the benefits that accrue from better student engagement and enhanced student performance outweigh this real, but limited, difficulty.

References

Cortright, R. N., Collins, H. L., Rodenbaugh, D. W., and DiCarlo, S. E. "Student Retention of Course Content Is Improved by Collaborative Group Testing." *Advances in Physiology Education*, 2003, 27, 102–108.

Michaelson, L. K., Knight, A. B., and Fink, L. D. (eds.). *Team-Based Learning: A Transformative Use of Small Groups*. Westport, Conn.: Praeger, 2002.

Millis, B. J., and Cottell, P. G. *Cooperative Learning for Higher Education Faculty*. Phoenix: American Council on Education and Oryx Press, 1998.

Nelson, C. "On the Persistence of Unicorns: The Trade-Off Between Content and Critical Thinking Revisited." In B. A. Pescosolido and R. Aminzade (eds.), *The Social Worlds of Higher Education: Handbook for Teaching in a New Century*. Thousand Oaks, Calif.: Pine Forge Press, 1999.

Ochoa, S., and others. "Improved Learning by Collaborative Testing." *Journal of Student Centered Learning*, 2004, 1, 127–140.

Seymour, E., and Hewitt, N. M. *Talking About Leaving: Why Undergraduates Leave the Sciences*. Boulder, Colo.: Westview Press, 1997.

Tobias, S. *They're Not Dumb, They're Different: Stalking the Second Tier*. Tucson, Ariz.: Research Corporation, 1994.

Tobias, S., and Raphael, J. *The Hidden Curriculum: Faculty Made Tests in Science: Part I Lower Division Courses*. New York: Plenum, 1997a.

Tobias, S., and Raphael, J. *The Hidden Curriculum: Faculty Made Tests in Science. Part II: Upper Division Courses*. New York: Plenum, 1997b.

Zull, J. E. *The Art of Changing the Brain*. Sterling, Va.: Stylus, 2002.

LINDA C. HODGES *is director of the Harold W. McGraw Jr. Center for Teaching and Learning at Princeton University in Princeton, New Jersey.*

In the project described in this chapter, discussions
during group exams were analyzed to gain insight into
how students make group decisions for their answers
and the implications of their decision-making methods
for deepening student understanding.

Making Student Thinking Visible by Examining Discussion During Group Testing

Theresa Castor

In my upper-division organizational communication class, I had long wondered how well my students understood the course material. Although the students performed adequately on assignments such as case study analyses and written assignments responding to the course readings, I was uncertain of how well they could actually think and talk in terms of the course concepts. I was unsure of what kind of ownership they had of the concepts. One day I decided to give the students a surprise multiple-choice quiz that was not graded but could help them to earn extra credit, and I had the students work in small groups.

For the first time during the semester, I had lively small group discussions of students engaging each other in the course concepts, explaining ideas to each other, and relating them to examples. This experience provided the basis for a more systematic research project the following semester on small-group discussions.

My general purpose here is to report on my project analyzing student discussions during small-group exams. I describe how students make decisions during group exams by analyzing their videotaped discussions. In

This project was possible through the assistance of Jim Robinson, Chuck Hiertz, and Linda Wawiorka of the University of Wisconsin-Parkside Instructional Technology Support. Fay Akindes and Wendy Leeds-Hurwitz provided feedback on early drafts of this chapter.

doing so, I outline procedures for group testing, advocate the benefits of group testing for student learning, and provide suggestions for other instructors on how to use this method to fuller advantage. I also provide cautionary notes regarding the limitations of group testing.

Learning as an Interactive, Constructive Process

Cooper and Robinson (2000) identify several benefits of small-group learning in the classroom, such as promoting cognitive elaboration, enhancing critical thinking, and providing feedback. A key assumption is that students learn when they are encouraged to articulate and explain their understanding to others and, in turn, when they must evaluate and respond to others (Smith and MacGregor, 1992).

Group testing lies within the realm of collaborative and cooperative learning. These ways of learning are premised on a constructivist view of knowledge in which students are seen as active rather than passive participants in their own learning process. Moreover, learning and interaction or "conversation" are interconnected in that "we think because we can talk, and we think in ways we have learned to talk" (Bruffee, 1992, p. 26). Students may also learn through the process of group testing by having to articulate their reasoning to other students and, in turn, by listening to and critically evaluating the reasoning of their peers.

Project Context

For this project, I worked with my Organizational Communication class, an upper-division class with about thirty students. My key method of assessing student learning of course concepts was through three quizzes. The quizzes consisted primarily of twelve to fifteen multiple-choice and one to two short-answer questions.

To prepare and motivate students for taking quizzes in groups, I used several in-class, ungraded exercises that illustrated the benefits of group synergy. For example, in one exercise they had to identify the number of squares in a diagram. They did this first individually and then working in small groups. Typically, the groups were closer to the correct answer than individuals, and the class soon realized this through a debriefing discussion after the activity.

In another exercise, the students completed short trivia quizzes individually and then in small groups using a variety of decision-making procedures such as dividing responsibility for answering questions, majority vote, and collaborative discussion. The scores on the trivia quizzes using each of these decision-making methods were placed on the chalkboard. The students immediately could see that the scores in which groups used collaboration were the highest. This activity, conducted in a safe space for students because it was not graded, illustrated for students the power of collaboration. This activity also functioned to alleviate students' anxiety regarding group testing by showing how groups can perform better than individuals for a given task.

Procedures for Testing

During the actual quiz-taking situation, students first had twenty minutes to take the quiz individually and then handed in their answer sheet. They were allowed to keep the quiz question sheet and encouraged to mark their answers on that sheet to assist them in the group portion. Students then took the same quiz in small groups of five to seven, completing a group answer sheet. The groups were formed in the preceding class period based on self-selection. Students had fifty minutes to complete the quiz as a group. The discussions of the groups were videotaped and then analyzed to identify patterns in how groups made decisions regarding the best answer for each question.

Student grades were based on adding individual scores with group scores. Both scores contributed to a student's grade in order to develop individual accountability and to discourage students from freeloading off the knowledge of their group members. However, when individuals scored higher than the group, they received double their score so that they would not feel that the group dragged down their score. Although there are other methods available for calculating grades for group tests (see Millis and Cottell, 1998), after discussion with a colleague assisting me with this project, I opted for simply adding the individual and group scores because this was the clearest method to explain to students and emphasized equally the importance of individual and group accountability.

Assessment of the Group Testing Format

Consistent with previous studies on group testing, the group scores were higher than the individual scores. There were only four instances over the three quizzes among the six groups in class in which an individual scored higher than his or her group. Although this quantitative information was encouraging, I wanted to gain a greater understanding of the group discussion process and how student groups determined their quiz responses.

In reviewing the videotapes, I identified the following ways in which the groups discussed the questions and their answers. Students tended to first use decision making by majority rule when deciding which answer was best. This entailed going around the group to find out which multiple-choice option each person selected. If there was a consensus, then the group would put down that answer and proceed to the next question.

Students would discuss the questions in more depth when there was a greater discrepancy in their answers or a lack of consensus or conviction behind a particular answer. During these discussions, students supported their answers through referencing examples discussed in class, textbook readings, personal study notes, or knowledge from prior classes. Some students, however, were less concrete in supporting their answers or did not provide a reason for their answers, and these statements were less persuasive to their peers.

When there was greater discussion, students seemed to discuss the question almost as much as they did the answer. In other words, students would explain the questions to each other to understand what was the most appropriate answer. There was also more in-depth discussion of the short-answer questions. However, this depth did not translate itself into the actual writing on the group quiz response.

Despite the encouraging quantitative results and positive student sentiments regarding group testing, there were also some limitations with this format for assessment. Most notably, during a focus group discussion conducted by a colleague, the class noted that they did not feel that the multiple-choice questions had them apply critical thinking. This sentiment is not surprising given the dominant use of majority rule for determining answers. For most questions, students did not have to think critically because members reached consensus quickly. Students also did not like the short-answer questions because of the challenge of composing a group answer.

Reflection and Suggestions for Future Instructors

Because of the potential newness of group testing as a means of assessment, an instructor should prepare students for taking quizzes in groups through prior exercises that illustrate the benefits and process of collaboration and group discussion. Preparation may involve using in-class ungraded activities that can show comparisons between individual and group efforts.

Given the amount of time students may spend on explaining the questions to each other during the quiz, students should be allowed to work in small groups during class or encouraged to work in small study groups out of class to discuss the concepts and notes on the study guide. After the first quiz, I implemented the practice of reviewing the study guide with the students and letting groups study together the class period before the exam.

Although student groups tended to score higher than individuals, there is a limited amount of thinking that students are required to do to perform well on the group quizzes. Whereas the ideal learning situation is for students to discuss each answer thoroughly, majority rule works sufficiently, and therefore, students tend to rely on this decision-making procedure unless there is not a majority convergence on a single answer. Another limitation of group testing is that it privileges individuals who are native-language speakers and who are more outspoken. Typically, there was an uneven amount of participation in the group.

In summary, in addition to providing a means for testing student knowledge, I have found that group quizzes are learning opportunities for students.

Through the testing situation, students may teach each other during the process of explaining and justifying their answers and, in turn, further their own understanding by having to provide explanations to their peers.

References

Bruffee, K. A. "Collaborative Learning and the 'Conversation of Mankind.'" In A. Goodsell, M. Maher, and V. Tinto (eds.), *Collaborative Learning: A Sourcebook for Higher Education*. University Park, Pa.: National Center on Postsecondary Teaching, Learning, and Assessment, 1992.

Cooper, J. L., and Robinson, P. "The Argument for Making Large Classes Seem Small." In J. MacGregor, J. L. Cooper, K. A. Smith, and P. Robinson (eds.), *Strategies for Energizing Large Classes: From Small Groups to Learning Communities*. New Directions for Teaching and Learning, no. 81. San Francisco: Jossey-Bass, 2000.

Millis, B. J., and Cottell, P. G. *Cooperative Learning for Higher Education Faculty*. Phoenix: American Council on Education and Oryx Press, 1998.

Smith, B. L., and MacGregor, J. T. "What Is Collaborative Learning?" In A. Goodsell, M. Maher, and V. Tinto (eds.), *Collaborative Learning: A Sourcebook for Higher Education*. University Park, Pa.: National Center on Postsecondary Teaching, Learning, and Assessment, 1992.

THERESA CASTOR is assistant professor of communication at the University of Wisconsin-Parkside and a 2003–2004 Wisconsin Teaching Fellow.

*The two models for group exams described here
employ these exams as both a formative strategy for
assessing student understanding of key course material
and preparing students for further class activities and
a summative strategy for evaluating student learning
and assigning grades.*

Two Examples of Group Exams from Communication and Engineering

Karin L. Sandell, Lonnie Welch

Often new methods of assessment must be adapted rather than adopted as a whole. This is particularly the case when we consider disciplinary differences in goals, epistemologies, and traditions. When we each decided to try the new idea of group exams in our respective courses, we found that adapting the general model to our situations was a challenge but a learning experience. Each of the two group testing models we eventually arrived at is discussed in terms of its rationale for use and strategies for implementation.

Rationale for Using Group Exams

The courses described in this analysis have a variety of reasons for using group exams. These reasons are discussed below.

Political Communication. This course provides students with an introduction to political communication, a broad sweep of topics representing the varying foci of the courses making up a certificate program. The course focus thus becomes the generating of questions and reflecting on answers rather than the mastery of specific content. Having freshman and sophomore students come to class prepared remains a problem, as do engaging students actively in the material and using the readings as a jumping-off point for discussion and problem solving. Although students would enthusiastically participate in the class activities, their lack of preparation, combined with difficulty in assessing their understanding of the material, made successful problem-solving exercises difficult to implement. Individual exams did not prepare students to participate in a meaningful way in group discussions, nor did they assess the students' preparedness for the exercises.

Software Engineering. The purpose of this course is to provide students with skills needed in the software engineering profession. Although they have completed numerous courses requiring the development of software, they typically lack several important perspectives, having focused almost exclusively on the implementation phase of software development, which is only one step in the modern software development processes employed by software engineering professionals. This is not a lecture-based course; the professor is not a "sage on the stage" but a "guide on the side." Student learning in the course is typically high, but students must take responsibility for their own learning. The teaching methods that are used to facilitate learning include the application of course material to case-study problems, "writing to learn," discussion, problem-based learning, and cooperative learning. These techniques result in deep learning and increased knowledge retention, but they also require students to be prepared, present, and engaged in all class meetings.

Role of Group Exams. Group exams are well suited for both of these contexts for at least three reasons. First, group exams are used to motivate students to prepare for class. Because little lecturing is done in class, it is essential that students keep up with the reading material. Thus, at the start of each class session, an exam is administered to encourage reading. The second reason that group exams are used is that they are an active learning strategy. During the group exam, students learn the material more deeply, and they learn from each other. They frequently debate their answers to the exam questions, which forces them to think about why they believe that their answers are correct. The group exam setting forces them to justify their answers to a knowledgeable and critical audience. Through the discussion during the exam, students have a chance to discuss things that may have been unclear to them and often teach each other. Third, group exams provide students with an opportunity to develop teamwork skills. The students are forced to resolve conflicts about answers to questions. Furthermore, they have an opportunity to apply knowledge about group dynamics and group roles that they learn in the course.

Group Exam Implementation

The implementation of the group exam in each of these classes was aimed at providing students with a substantive mutual-learning experience that engaged them in the reading materials and provided the instructor with an assessment of their understanding of key concepts. In both courses, the instructor uses an individual exam to stimulate student thinking and reduce social loafing, followed immediately by the same exam completed by the group. By the end of this process, everyone in the class knows the materials thoroughly and is prepared to spend the remaining class time on projects and other work. In addition, the instructor has a good sense of remaining gaps in student understanding and can fill those gaps in before proceeding to projects and other work.

The process used for implementing group exams in each of the classes is similar, as follows: First, as students arrive for class, they receive an individual copy of the exam covering that evening's material. This exam serves two purposes: (1) a major part of the students' grades for the exam depends on their individual achievement, thus ensuring individual accountability; and (2) each student has reflected critically on the course material before moving into the group exam stage, thus preparing for the group process that follows. After turning in the individual exam, the students retake the exam in groups. During the group exam session, students discuss and justify their answers to the exam questions. One can often observe a member of a group teaching concepts to the other members of the group.

Students in both of these courses receive immediate feedback after taking the test. A teaching assistant in computer science, for example, grades the group exams during the remainder of the class session, and the graded exams are returned before the students leave. In the political communication course, individual exams are graded while team exams are taken; this provides the instructor with information about individual gaps and confusion in student learning to that point. For the group part of the exam, an Immediate Feedback Assessment Technique (IF-AT) form is used, thus resulting in immediate feedback to group members on multiple-choice questions. The IF-AT, designed by Epstein (2004), provides a scratch-off answer form for use with exams that employ multiple-choice questions. Students scratch off what they believe to be the correct response and receive immediate feedback when they discover—or fail to discover—a symbol indicating they have made the correct choice. They can keep choosing until they find the correct response. After students have made an initial wrong choice, they tend to be extremely careful in making the next one because the form is scored to reflect the number of tries taken in locating the correct response. Additional questions are scored by the instructor.

One additional step in the political communication course allows the groups to write an appeal that addresses their rationale for choosing a different answer from the one designated as correct by the instructor. This has proved at times to be the most engaging part of the process for students as they critically examine their reasoning versus the reasoning of the instructor. Although some of the appeals remain unsubstantiated by the course materials, others thoughtfully connect previous reading and course materials in ways that persuade the instructor to rethink the whole question and award points.

Issues in Implementation

A number of issues need to be resolved when implementing group exams, including the formation of groups, the division of points between individual and group exams, and engaging students in the process.

Group Formation. Each class is based on a lot of group work, and one issue in each has been whether to compose exam groups that are different from team project groups, thus giving students a chance to work with different sets of students. Using different teams for different purposes makes the dynamics of the class more interesting for the students and provides additional opportunities for the students to develop teamwork and leadership skills. In both cases, the exam groups remain constant throughout the quarter. Following principles of cooperative learning, these formal exam groups develop loyalty among members, thus adding to the incentive to come prepared and not let the other members down. In addition, the developing relationship among exam team members may lead to decisions to study together outside of class, a desired outcome of both courses. The group size remains small, with three members assigned to exam groups to maximize participation.

Scoring the Exams. A number of different models exist for scoring the exams. Weimer (2004) reports, for example, that she computes an average score for the group members and then adds to each individual score the difference between that average and the group exam score. For both of the courses described here, 75 percent of the final exam grade is determined by the individual performance, with the remaining 25 percent derived from the group performance. In all cases, the larger portion of the score comes from individual work, providing motivation for independent study and preparation. A danger of having a larger percentage come from the group work could be that some students would opt to come unprepared and depend on the group score to raise their grade on the exam. Furthermore, no student is penalized with a lower score in the rare case where the group outcome does not exceed an individual score.

Incentive for Participating. From a student's perspective, the incentive in the process remains the extrinsic reward in the form of grades (although students also become more engaged in the process as they become more familiar with it). To demonstrate differences between group and individual performance, in hopes of influencing students' acceptance of the process, the first day of both the political communication and the software engineering class includes an exam—but only on the syllabus. These exams are taken first individually and then in teams, and students are prompted to report the differences between their individual scores and the scores of the groups in which they are working. With rare exceptions, the groups outscore the individuals every time, thus demonstrating to students the value of the group exam process.

Conclusion

By the completion of the group exam, students are well versed in the material. They have studied, taken an individual exam, then discussed and argued about it as a group. At the end of the exam cycle, they know what they know with confidence, and the instructor knows what gaps or misconceptions remain that need addressing. The rest of the class period remains open for application and extension of the initial concepts covered in the readings.

References

Epstein, M. "Immediate Feedback Assessment Technique." n.d. Retrieved June 3, 2004, from http://epsteineducation.com/how.php.

Weimer, M. "Teaching That Promotes Learning." Public address, Ohio University at Athens, Spotlight on Learning, Mar. 5, 2004.

KARIN L. SANDELL is director of the Center for Teaching Excellence at Ohio University at Athens.

LONNIE WELCH is in the Department of Electrical Engineering and Computer Science at Ohio University at Athens.

PART FIVE

Improving Assessment by Improving the Students

Daily practice tests over assigned reading followed immediately by class discussion can improve learning and grades.

Using Practice Tests on a Regular Basis to Improve Student Learning

Margaret K. Snooks

Our seven-thousand-student campus is located near a major metropolitan area. Most students are nontraditional: they are older, employed, married commuters. Often they are the first generation in their families to attend college. Classes are upper level, so students have had at least two years of college-level experience. Nevertheless, they are anxious about grades and interested in guidance to improve learning.

Five years ago, faculty members began visiting each other's classes at midterm and asking students how courses were going (Snooks, Neeley, and Williamson, 2004). Clearly, students worried most about examinations, specifically, about what was going to be tested from reading assignments. Their response to "What would improve your learning?" was for faculty members to explicitly say what was important in readings. Students commented, "There is so much material to read and study, it is difficult to know what is important." Such statements surfaced regardless of the course or major. The most alarmed students faced one comprehensive examination that determined their entire grade.

Research shows that anxiety interferes with learning and performance. Nontraditional college students report being stressed by classes, jobs, and families. Grade anxiety tops their list of school-related stressors. The damaging effects of stress on physical, social, and emotional health are well documented. Anxiety disorders, including fears and phobias, often lead to avoidance behaviors such as dropping out of school. Many faculty members report nearly palpable distress and hostility when examinations and papers are returned to students. Anxiety can negatively affect academic performance in other ways. A study of medical students' stress by Kiecolt-Glaser,

Malarkey, Cacioppo, and Glaser (1994) documented reduced immune system competence with more infectious diseases among students following exams. Illness and absences further compound academic problems.

Development and Rationale for Using Practice Tests

Using practice tests was an effort to improve student learning and grades. An additional hope was to reduce student anxiety. The use of practice tests followed several other classroom innovations, including providing students with questions about reading assignments. Professors often complain that their students do not read texts. Providing chapter questions seemed one way to inform students about important points made in textbooks, points that would not be covered in class. Learning and grades were still disappointing, so using practice tests on a regular basis was initiated.

The pathway to students' benefiting from practice tests partially relates to self-efficacy theory, or the belief that one can successfully perform behaviors to achieve desired outcomes. The behavior is learning course material; the desired outcome is better grades. If students frequently took practice tests, they would learn more, self-efficacy would increase, test anxiety would be reduced, immune systems might benefit, and grades would improve. This logic also relates to stress-inoculation theory, whereby persons exposed to small doses of a frightening experience eventually experience less fear and anxiety.

The idea of using practice tests to facilitate student learning is intuitively appealing because for decades students have studied old exams. It seems logical that familiarity with various kinds of test items will improve learning. Students believe that practice tests are a beneficial review strategy (Kulik, Kulik, and Bangert, 1984). Thorne (2000) found that using extra-credit pop quizzes encouraged preparation for class. A study of computerized practice tests found a positive relationship between the number of practice exams taken and course grades, even when previous SAT scores were controlled (Gretes and Green, 2000). More than 90 percent of students reported that practice tests helped them study for "real" examinations.

Practice Test Routine

The routine, based on the research, includes short practice tests over reading assignments taken at the beginning of each class. Students first take the test alone. They then compare answers and discuss questions with neighbors. Finally, as a whole class, all questions are discussed, including what is the "best" answer and why it is superior to other answers. This process promotes critical-thinking, question-analysis, and test-taking skills that carry over to other classes and to life in general because people must answer written questions for job interviews, medical visits, credit applications, and so forth.

Practice tests are nonthreatening; all students get credit. Paramount is stimulating students to think and talk about important issues in addition to reading about them. The class discussions of practice tests often reveal student misunderstandings of issues in assigned readings. Records of practice tests substitute for roll calling, so more students come to class on time. The entire process takes about ten minutes. Knowledge increases, and skills are developed through immediate instructor feedback on each question.

For practice tests to be effective, faculty members must be clear about course objectives, including what is important in reading assignments. Textbooks, reading assignments, chapter questions, and practice tests should explicitly reflect course objectives, as should exam questions. Practice test questions must be academically sound, authentic, and important. This is not to be confused with drilling or teaching tests. Questions are similar in format and style to those used on examinations.

Benefits of Regular Practice Tests

There are benefits to practice tests in addition to encouraging students to come to class on time. Most important are increases in learning and students making better grades. This occurs for several reasons. First, knowledge and skills increase simply because students practice demonstrating knowledge and skills. Practice tests reinforce instructors' expectations related to reading assignments because students start with guiding questions about each chapter. Students are relieved to be given this direction.

Students also become familiar with different question formats. Sometimes practice questions check knowledge; other times they test for concept application. Furthermore, students receive immediate feedback on their knowledge so that they can better focus their studying. Test anxiety is reduced. Self-efficacy is increased. On a daily basis, students wrestle with questions covering knowledge and skills. By the time a real examination rolls around, students are eager to show what they know.

The student-instructor relationship also improves. The palpable hostility perceived on returning graded work has disappeared. Now, in going over examinations, a student may ask why "c" is the correct answer. Fellow students promptly explain why "c" is best and why other responses are not as good. Grades and testing often make students feel adversarial toward instructors who they describe as "tricky." With daily practice tests, students see instructors as guides pointing them in the right direction for learning. The instructor is no longer an obstacle to better grades. The entire class becomes oriented to learning.

Students take practice tests alone and then compare ideas with neighbors, so practice tests become collaborative activities. Students give and receive information daily. They talk about ideas in support of their thinking. Finally, discussing practice test answers, as a whole class, encourages more discussion. Rather than being embarrassed about their "ignorance," students feel safe saying, "*We* thought X was a better answer because ___." Learning reflects cultural, social, and individual experiences. Coming together as a whole class allows the consideration of issues from many different perspectives.

Evidence of Effectiveness

Enhanced student learning demonstrated through grade improvement is one measure of effectiveness of teaching innovations. Class records over three years show that practice tests improve students' grades. The more practice tests taken, the more likely students are to earn higher course grades. The reverse is also true: the fewer practice tests taken, the more likely a lower final grade. One might argue that practice tests merely measure attendance rather than increases in students' learning, but if an innovation encourages attendance, it is beneficial.

Student observations can also be used to evaluate teaching innovations. On course evaluations, students rank practice tests as "very helpful." By themselves, reading assignments are least likely to be ranked helpful. Anonymous end-of-semester responses to "What aspects of this course worked best for you?" always include " practice tests." Dropout rates and student end-of-course evaluations are additional effectiveness measures. Dropout rates are less than 1 percent. This year, the median student evaluation score was 4.9 out of 5.0.

Conclusion

When faced with poor academic performance, many instructors may believe that student demographics are the cause. This opinion is hardly helpful because faculty members can rarely influence characteristics of enrolled students. What can be controlled is the learning environment. Regular practice tests, as described here, focus attention on vital course content, promote reassurance about recent learning, and increase satisfaction with educational experiences. Any instructor disappointed with students' progress might consider using regular practice tests, followed immediately by whole-class discussions with instructor feedback.

References

Gretes, J. A., and Green, M. "Improving Undergraduate Learning with Computer-Assisted Assessment." *Journal of Research on Computing in Education,* 2000, *33*(1), 46–55.

Kiecolt-Glaser, J. K., Malarkey, W. B., Cacioppo, J. T., and Glaser, R. "Stressful Personal Relationships: Immune and Endocrine Function." In R. Glaser and J. K. Kiecolt-Glaser (eds.), *Handbook of Human Stress and Immunity.* San Diego, Calif.: Academic Press, 1994.

Kulik, J. A., Kulik, C. C., and Bangert, R. L. "Effects of Practice on Aptitude and Achievement Test Scores." *American Educational Research Journal*, 1984, 21(2), 435–447.

Snooks, M. K., Neeley, S. E., and Williamson, K. M. "From SGID and Gift to BBQ: Streamlining Midterm Student Evaluations to Improve Teaching and Learning." *To Improve the Academy*, 2004, 22, 110–124.

Thorne, B. M. "Extra Credit Exercise: A Painless Pop Quiz." *Teaching of Psychology*, 2000, 27(3), 204–206.

Margaret K. Snooks is co-convener of the University of Houston–Clear Lake Teaching-Learning Enhancement Center and a faculty member in the School of Human Sciences and Humanities.

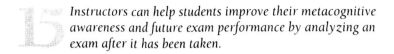

Instructors can help students improve their metacognitive awareness and future exam performance by analyzing an exam after it has been taken.

Post-Test Analysis: A Tool for Developing Students' Metacognitive Awareness and Self-Regulation

Michelle V. Achacoso

Examining test performance with students is a practice that is done in a variety of ways in college classrooms. Many times instructors return exams and go over the correct responses during class. Another common way students receive feedback on exam performance is to check their scores on course management systems, such as Blackboard, or to go see the teaching assistant during office hours. What is important is that at the postsecondary level, it is up to individual students to figure out why they performed a certain way on an exam. After looking at the score, most students put the test out of their mind and move on to the next academic task. However, analyzing one's performance provides a great opportunity to improve on future similar tasks. Explicitly teaching students to analyze their test performance can help them to better assess the understanding of their own cognitive process, or what is known as metacognitive awareness (Flavell, 1979). This means that when students become aware of what they do and do not know about specific content, they develop greater metacognitive awareness. This type of awareness can be helpful in fostering self-regulated learning in college students.

I developed a method to help my students understand their performance on an exam (Exhibit 15.1). The first step is to have them predict their exam score. I do this to help the students learn to gauge how well their perception of performance correlates with their effort. In the literature, this comparison is called calibration of performance. In general, there appears to be a positive relationship between an accurate calibration of performance

Exhibit 15.1. Exam Feedback Questions

Before you see your exam:
1. Please predict your score: (0–100 percent)
2. How much effort did you put into preparing for this exam?

1	2	3	4	5	6	7	8	9	10
Low effort				Moderate effort					High effort

3. How long did you study for the exam?
4. List the specific strategies you used to study for this exam.
5. What did you find easiest for you on the exam? Why?
6. What was most difficult for you on the exam? Why?

After you see your exam score:

7. Now that you have seen your exam, how do you feel about your performance? Was your prediction correct?
8. Did you experience the illusion of knowing? Why or why not?
9. Determine the level of Bloom's Taxonomy of the Cognitive Domain for each question.
10. Determine the percentages of right or wrong responses for each level of Bloom's.

	Percentage Correct	Percentage Incorrect
Knowledge		
Comprehension		
Application		
Analysis		
Synthesis		
Evaluation		

11. Determine the source of each test question: book, lecture, or both.
12. Determine the percentage of right or wrong responses for the book, lecture, or both.

	Percentage Correct	Percentage Incorrect
Book		
Lecture		
Both		

13. On the next exam in this class, would you change any of the strategies you used or the amount of time you spent studying? Please be specific.
14. Can you suggest anything else I as your instructor could do to help you to prepare for the exam?

Source: Developed by Michelle Achacoso, University of Texas Learning Center, 2004.

and achievement (Lin, Moore, and Zabrucky, 2001; Zabrucky and Moore, 1996). I use this method to help students become aware of their own perception of performance when they later compare their actual performance.

Next I have students rate their effort in studying for the exam on a scale of 1 to 10. At this point, students have a measure of perception of performance and effort. The first two steps in this process help students become conscious of their perception of performance and effort, and this will soon be juxtaposed with reality when the exams are returned. Consider a 2×2 matrix of "effort and performance" (Figure 15.1). It makes sense that students who

Figure 15.1. Effort Versus Performance

		Effort	
		Low	High
Performance	Low	This makes sense	Struggling student
	High	Outliers, anomalies	This makes sense

put in low effort do not perform well on an exam. Likewise, students who put in high effort perform well. Students who put in low effort and attain high performance are, more or less, anomalies. Certainly it happens, but this is not the group I am concerned about here. Students who put in high effort and do not perform well are students who are clearly struggling. This post-test analysis was designed to help these particular students.

I then have students list the specific learning strategies they used to study for the exam. Answering this question is key to helping a student develop more complex critical-thinking skills like analysis, synthesis, and evaluation. Students who use rehearsal strategies to simply memorize information might not be able to perform tasks that require a more complex level of cognitive functioning. For example, a student might put in a lot of effort (8 or 9 on the scale) studying for an exam, but he or she may simply rely on reviewing note cards and repetition. If the demands of the exam push the student to apply or analyze the material, rote memory devices might not be sufficient for the task at hand. A student might well need to use a more complex elaboration or organizational strategy to make the necessary connections to be ready for the exam.

Next I ask students what were the easiest and the most difficult aspects about the exam and why. I ask this question to learn whether perhaps there was a problem with the exam itself. Perhaps I asked a question in a vague manner or designed a poorly written question. This gives the student the opportunity to express such a grievance.

Next I have the students talk about their affective response to the exam after they see their score. It helps students to have a place to talk about their performance. Contrary to what might be expected, students were rarely inappropriate with expressing their feelings to me. In fact, more often than not, they were particularly hard on themselves if they did not live up to their own expectations.

I next have the students compare their score with their prediction and decide if their prediction was correct. Here students get to assess if they calibrated their performance properly. I also ask them if they experienced the illusion of knowing (Glenberg, Wilkinson, and Epstein, 1982). Students who experience the illusion of knowing feel confident that they performed well on an academic task, only to find out after completing a task that there was a gap in their understanding.

Helping a student identify this phenomenon when it occurs is particularly important for the development of the metacognitive skills of the student. Someone who experiences the illusion of knowing is generally sure that they knew the answers to an exam. The reality is that a student might have learned the information well enough to recognize terms on a multiple-choice test, for example, but the cognitive demands of the exam may have gone beyond the level of recognition.

At this point in the analysis process, I ask the students to identify the level of Bloom's "taxonomy of educational objectives" (Bloom, 1956) used in each question on the exam. I also ask them to calculate the proportion of items they answered correctly or incorrectly at each level of Bloom's classification. I do this to see if the students are preparing at the appropriate cognitive level to meet the demands of the exam. They may have been tested at the application level but only studied to perform at the knowledge level. It is easy to recognize something but much harder to understand, explain, apply, or analyze a complex concept. Accurate knowledge assessment is critical to developing metacognitive skills (Everson and Tobias, 1998). If students do not have an understanding of what they do and do not know, it is impossible for them to make needed repairs in their knowledge.

After conducting a Bloom's analysis, I also have the students determine the source of each question: book, lecture, or both. I ask them to do this to determine where they might need to focus more of their attention for future exams. If they are skipping class and much of the exam comes from the lectures, this is a signal to come to lecture. In the same vein, students can also check to see if they need to be reading the book more carefully.

Next I ask students if they would make any changes in strategies or perhaps in the amount of time they will spend studying for the next exam. Asking this question helps students find the appropriate attribution for their performance. For example, if students believe they have control over the outcome, they are more likely to be motivated to make a change. Of course, it is easy to blame an instructor or the exam itself for a failure in performance. This question helps students realize the role they play in their own grades. As a consequence, students were less likely to argue about a grade with me after going through this process.

Finally, I asked for any suggestions they had about helping them prepare for the next exam. Students generally gave constructive feedback on what I could do to help. They did not say things like "just tell us what is on the test." I would always try to integrate their feedback during the next review to show them that I took their feedback seriously.

Post-test analysis helped me to accomplish three important outcomes in my teaching: First, the process helped to increase metacognitive awareness in my students. By the end of the semester, they were able to monitor and make changes in their strategy used when studying for exams. Students improved in their performance. The class mean on each exam increased as the semester progressed. Second, motivation increased due to making more appropriate attributions about exam performance. Students could see how their effort and strategy used were directly related to performance. Third, "grade groveling" was kept to a minimum during my office hours, and the adversarial relationship between the instructor and student was definitely minimized. The students saw that I was willing to listen to their opinions, incorporate their feedback, and change my approach to help them learn.

References

Bloom, B. S. *Taxonomy of Educational Objectives: The Classification of Educational Goals. Handbook 1: Cognitive Domain.* New York: McKay, 1956.

Everson, H. T., and Tobias, S. "The Ability to Estimate Knowledge and Performance in College: A Metacognitive Analysis." *Instructional Science,* 1998, 26(1–2), 65–79.

Flavell, J. H. "Metacognition and Cognitive Monitoring: A New Area of Cognitive-Developmental Inquiry." *American Psychologist,* 1979, 34(10), 906–911.

Glenberg, A. M., Wilkinson, A. C., and Epstein, W. "The Illusion of Knowing: Failure in Self-Assessment of Comprehension." *Memory and Cognition,* 1982, 10, 597–602.

Lin, L. M., Moore, D., and Zabrucky, K. M. "An Assessment of Students' Calibration of Comprehension and Calibration of Performance Using Multiple Measures." *Reading Psychology,* 2001, 22, 111–128.

Zabrucky, K., and Moore, D. "College Students' Use of Different Standards to Evaluate Understanding." *Reading Psychology,* 1996, 17(4), 285–307.

MICHELLE V. ACHACOSO is director of research at the University of Texas Learning Center in Austin.

INDEX

Back Issue/Subscription Order Form

Copy or detach and send to:

Jossey-Bass, A Wiley Imprint, 989 Market Street, San Francisco CA 94103-1741

Call or fax toll-free: Phone 888-378-2537 6:30AM – 3PM PST; Fax 888-481-2665

Back Issues: Please send me the following issues at $27 each
(Important: please include ISBN number with your order.)

_____

_____

_____

$ _____   Total for single issues

$ _____   SHIPPING CHARGES: SURFACE   Domestic Canadian
                                 First Item $5.00 $6.00
                                 Each Add'l Item $3.00 $1.50
                 For next-day and second-day delivery rates, call the number listed above.

Subscriptions   Please __ start __ renew my subscription to *New Directions for
                 Teaching and Learning* for the year 2___ at the following rate:

                 U.S.   __ Individual $80   __ Institutional $170
                 Canada   __ Individual $80   __ Institutional $210
                 All Others   __ Individual $104   __ Institutional $244

                 **For more information about online subscriptions visit
                 www.interscience.wiley.com**

$ _____   Total single issues and subscriptions (Add appropriate sales tax
                 for your state for single issue orders. No sales tax for U.S.
                 subscriptions. Canadian residents, add GST for subscriptions and
                 single issues.)

__Payment enclosed (U.S. check or money order only)
__VISA __ MC __ AmEx #_____ Exp. Date _____

Signature _____ Day Phone _____
__ Bill Me (U.S. institutional orders only. Purchase order required.)

Purchase order # _____
                 Federal Tax ID13559302   **GST 89102 8052**

Name _____

Address _____

_____

Phone _____ E-mail _____

For more information about Jossey-Bass, visit our Web site at www.josseybass.com

their own education by actively interpreting information. Today's professors are adopting problem-based learning across all disciplines to faciliate a broader, modern definition of what it means to learn. Authors provide practical experience about designing useful problems, creating conducive learning environments, facilitating students' activities, and assessing students' efforts at problem solving.
ISBN: 0-7879-7172-3

TL94   **Technology: Taking the Distance out of Learning**
Margit Misangyi Watts
This volume addresses the possibilities and challenges of computer technology in higher education. The contributors examine the pressures to use technology, the reasons not to, the benefits of it, the feeling of being a learner as well as a teacher, the role of distance education, and the place of computers in the modern world. Rather than discussing only specific successes or failures, this issue addresses computers as a new cultural symbol and begins meaningful conversations about technology in general and how it affects education in particular.
ISBN: 0-7879-6989-3

TL93   **Valuing and Supporting Undergraduate Research**
Joyce Kinkead
The authors gathered in this volume share a deep belief in the value of undergraduate research. Research helps students develop skills in problem solving, critical thinking, and communication, and undergraduate researchers' work can contribute to an institution's quest to further knowledge and help meet societal challenges. Chapters provide an overview of undergraduate research, explore programs at different types of institutions, and offer suggestions on how faculty members can find ways to work with undergraduate researchers.
ISBN: 0-7879-6907-9

TL92   **The Importance of Physical Space in Creating Supportive Learning Environments**
Nancy Van Note Chism, Deborah J. Bickford
The lack of extensive dialogue on the importance of learning spaces in higher education environments prompted the essays in this volume. Chapter authors look at the topic of learning spaces from a variety of perspectives, elaborating on the relationship between physical space and learning, arguing for an expanded notion of the concept of learning spaces and furnishings, talking about the context within which decision making for learning spaces takes place, and discussing promising approaches to the renovation of old learning spaces and the construction of new ones.
ISBN: 0-7879-6344-5

TL91   **Assessment Strategies for the On-Line Class: From Theory to Practice**
Rebecca S. Anderson, John F. Bauer, Bruce W. Speck
Addresses the kinds of questions that instructors need to ask themselves as they begin to move at least part of their students' work to an on-line format. Presents an initial overview of the need for evaluating students' on-line work with the same care that instructors give to the work in hard-copy format. Helps guide instructors who are considering using on-line learning in conjunction with their regular classes, as well as those interested in going totally on-line.
ISBN: 0-7879-6343-7

TL90 Scholarship in the Postmodern Era: New Venues, New Values, New Visions
Kenneth J. Zahorski
A little over a decade ago, Ernest Boyer's *Scholarship Reconsidered* burst upon the academic scene, igniting a robust national conversation that maintains its vitality to this day. This volume aims at advancing that important conversation. Its first section focuses on the new settings and circumstances in which the act of scholarship is being played out; its second identifies and explores the fresh set of values currently informing today's scholarly practices; and its third looks to the future of scholarship, identifying trends, causative factors, and potentialities that promise to shape scholars and their scholarship in the new millennium.
ISBN: 0-7879-6293-7

TL89 Applying the Science of Learning to University Teaching and Beyond
Diane F. Halpern, Milton D. Hakel
Seeks to build on empirically validated learning activities to enhance what and how much is learned and how well and how long it is remembered. Demonstrates that the movement for a real science of learning—the application of scientific principles to the study of learning—has taken hold both under the controlled conditions of the laboratory and in the messy real-world settings where most of us go about the business of teaching and learning.
ISBN: 0-7879-5791-7

TL88 Fresh Approaches to the Evaluation of Teaching
Christopher Knapper, Patricia Cranton
Describes a number of alternative approaches, including interpretive and critical evaluation, use of teaching portfolios and teaching awards, performance indicators and learning outcomes, technology-mediated evaluation systems, and the role of teacher accreditation and teaching scholarship in instructional evaluation.
ISBN: 0-7879-5789-5

TL87 Techniques and Strategies for Interpreting Student Evaluations
Karron G. Lewis
Focuses on all phases of the student rating process—from data-gathering methods to presentation of results. Topics include methods of encouraging meaningful evaluations, mid-semester feedback, uses of quality teams and focus groups, and creating questions that target individual faculty needs and interest.
ISBN: 0-7879-5789-5

TL86 Scholarship Revisited: Perspectives on the Scholarship of Teaching
Carolin Kreber
Presents the outcomes of a Delphi Study conducted by an international panel of academics working in faculty evaluation scholarship and postsecondary teaching and learning. Identifies the important components of scholarship of teaching, defines its characteristics and outcomes, and explores its most pressing issues.
ISBN: 0-7879-5447-0

TL85 Beyond Teaching to Mentoring
Alice G. Reinarz, Eric R. White
Offers guidelines to optimizing student learning through classroom activities as well as peer, faculty, and professional mentoring. Addresses mentoring

techniques in technical training, undergraduate business, science, and liberal arts studies, health professions, international study, and interdisciplinary work.
ISBN: 0-7879-5617-1

TL84   **Principles of Effective Teaching in the Online Classroom**
Renée E. Weiss, Dave S. Knowlton, Bruce W. Speck
Discusses structuring the online course, utilizing resources from the World Wide Web and using other electronic tools and technology to enhance classroom efficiency. Addresses challenges unique to the online classroom community, including successful communication strategies, performance evaluation, academic integrity, and accessibility for disabled students.
ISBN: 0-7879-5615-5

TL83   **Evaluating Teaching in Higher Education: A Vision for the Future**
Katherine E. Ryan
Analyzes the strengths and weaknesses of current approaches to evaluating teaching and recommends practical strategies for improving current evaluation methods and developing new ones. Provides an overview of new techniques such as peer evaluations, portfolios, and student ratings of instructors and technologies.
ISBN: 0-7879-5448-9

TL82   **Teaching to Promote Intellectual and Personal Maturity: Incorporating Students' Worldviews and Identities into the Learning Process**
Marcia B. Baxter Magolda
Explores cognitive and emotional dimensions that influence how individuals learn, and describes teaching practices for building on these to help students develop intellectually and personally. Examines how students' unique understanding of their individual experience, themselves, and the ways knowledge is constructed can mediate learning.
ISBN: 0-7879-5446-2

NEW DIRECTIONS FOR TEACHING AND LEARNING IS NOW AVAILABLE ONLINE AT WILEY INTERSCIENCE

What is Wiley InterScience?

Wiley InterScience is the dynamic online content service from John Wiley & Sons delivering the full text of over 300 leading scientific, technical, medical, and professional journals, plus major reference works, the acclaimed Current Protocols laboratory manuals, and even the full text of select Wiley print books online.

What are some special features of Wiley InterScience?

Wiley Interscience Alerts is a service that delivers table of contents via e-mail for any journal available on Wiley InterScience as soon as a new issue is published online.
EarlyView is Wiley's exclusive service presenting individual articles online as soon as they are ready, even before the release of the compiled print issue. These articles are complete, peer-reviewed, and citable.
CrossRef is the innovative multi-publisher reference linking system enabling readers to move seamlessly from a reference in a journal article to the cited publication, typically located on a different server and published by a different publisher.

How can I access Wiley InterScience?

Visit http://www.interscience.wiley.com.

Guest Users can browse Wiley InterScience for unrestricted access to journal tables of contents and article abstracts, or use the powerful search engine.
Registered Users are provided with a *Personal Home Page* to store and manage customized alerts, searches, and links to favorite journals and articles. Additionally, Registered Users can view free online sample issues and preview selected material from major reference works.
Licensed Customers are entitled to access full-text journal articles in PDF, with select journals also offering full-text HTML.

How do I become an Authorized User?

Authorized Users are individuals authorized by a paying Customer to have access to the journals in Wiley InterScience. For example, a university that subscribes to Wiley journals is considered to be the Customer.
Faculty, staff and students authorized by the university to have access to those journals in Wiley InterScience are Authorized Users. Users should contact their library for information on which Wiley journals they have access to in Wiley InterScience.

ASK YOUR INSTITUTION ABOUT WILEY INTERSCIENCE TODAY!

Printed in the United States
85906LV00004B/299/A

9 780787 979706